Praise for L

"Lifted will take you on a journey—a journey to be your best self, a journey to recognize what is holding you back, a journey to be who you want to be in every important moment."

—Cindy Monroe, founder and CEO of Thirty-One Gifts

"Reading Lindsey's story helps you to see your life in a new light. Her raw honesty makes you feel as though you aren't alone in life's toughest moments, and her strong faith and heart pull you close and keep you wanting more."

—Megan Lieb, CEO of Who Does Your Hair?, Ltd., inspirational blogger

"Lindsey has created and shared her brilliant approach to day-to-day living in her book, *Lifted*. I have seen Lindsey's incredible courage, passion, authenticity, and humor in action as she has walked this journey in her marriage, motherhood, friendships, and leadership roles. Lindsey is a game changer, and after reading this book, you will be too! This is a must-read for every woman."

—Andrea Dowding, executive coach and author

"Lindsey is passionate about changing the lives of women around her! This book is a testimony to her passion, humor, and ability to relate to women authentically."

—Jill Savage, author of *No More Perfect Moms*

"Lindsey is an authentic encourager of pursuing your dreams and helping you find who God created you to be! If you've ever struggled with love and acceptance—this book is for you!"

—Nicki Green, pastor of involvement, Eastview Christian Church

"Lindsey's ability to relate to women is unmatched. I have watched her share her raw experiences with women from all walks of life and draw people in with grace and acceptance.

"She will encourage you to reflect upon the critical moments in your own life that have shaped who you are today. I love that Lindsey challenges you to welcome change as an old friend rather than with fear. You will be *lifted* after reading this book. It is a call to action for living your best life!"

—Janel Miner, personal fitness trainer and wellness coach

"Lindsey's vulnerability, life experiences, and humor make this a must-read for women who want to live life to the fullest!"

—Martine Williams, empowerment and confidence coach, creator of the Choose You course

Lifted

How to Ditch Fear, Obligation, and Guilt and Live *Your* Best Life

Lindsey J. Hale

These books are available at special discounts when purchased in bulk for use as premiums, promotions, fundraising, or group studies. For inquiries and details, contact us: info@courageousheartpress.com.

Published by Courageous Heart Press
CourageousHeartPress.com

Library of Congress Control Number: 2019939119
Paperback ISBN: 978-0-9969984-9-9
Ebook ISBN: 978-1-950714-00-1

First Printing: May 2019

Contents

Foreword ix

Chapter 1: Say No to Normal. 1

Chapter 2: Liar, Liar. 7

Chapter 3: Fear of Missing Out. 13

Chapter 4: The Great Comeback. 27

Chapter 5: What Successful Women Do Differently. . . . 35

Chapter 6: Take Off the Mask 43

Chapter 7: Shiny Spots 49

Chapter 8: Finding the Right Relationships. 63

Chapter 9: Building Boundaries .79

Chapter 10: Princess of Power—Choose You! 91

Chapter 11: Grace Over Guilt. 105

Chapter 12: When Opportunity Knocks ... Ask for
                   Identification. 115

Chapter 13: Forgiving Your Way to Transformation. . . . 123

About the Author 135

Foreword

Cindy Monroe, founder/CEO, Thirty-One Gifts

I'm so honored to introduce you to Lindsey Hale and her *passion* for helping you find and live your best life. When you know Lindsey—her heart, her passion, and what drives her—it's easy to understand her success leading and impacting women. Lindsey and I have several things in common, but the one thing that stands out the most is our ability to get up when we have been knocked down.

Who among us hasn't felt knocked down at one time or another?

If you are feeling as if life has knocked you down and you want to get back up, then this is the book for you. The way Lindsey shares her life stories will have you laughing and crying, and her insights will help you discover how you got to where you are and how to get where you want to be.

When I first read her acronym of FOG, I had to pause. *Fear, obligation,* and *guilt* have knocked me down and held me back—time and time again. Lindsey's personal story related to my own in many ways, and in at least once instance, I was reminded how different a person I am today than I was even a few years ago. Her vulnerability allowed me to realize that we can overcome fear, obligations, and guilt to find a full life as we relentlessly chase after all that God has for us.

Lifted will take you on a journey—a journey to be your best self, a journey to recognize what is holding you back, a journey to be who you want to be in every important moment.

Thank you, Lindsey, for loving me and for reminding me to love others well and to love God's calling—even when I question it.

What a privilege to share Lindsey Hale and her book *Lifted* with all of you! Don't be afraid to find clarity and live your best life.

Are you ready to find your way out of life's FOG? Download the *Lifted* Study Guide at LindseyHale.org and use it as you read through this book.

Chapter 1
Say No to Normal

I had everything I'd ever wanted, so why did I cry myself to sleep every night? As a young girl, I spent nights cutting out pictures and pasting them to my school folders. The wish-filled collages, including the happy wedding, a beautiful family, a house on a tree-lined street, and an adorable dog, had become my reality. Now, in my late twenties, I had it all: I'd married my high school sweetheart, we had two precious children, a yellow lab, and a house in a great neighborhood. But somehow, I felt as if I were no longer in the picture. I had completely lost myself in the process of fulfilling those dreams.

My picture-perfect life was anything but. Instead, it felt completely average and unsatisfying. Finances were tight, and marriage was hard, especially with children added into the mix. I'd had two babies in less than two years, which meant I was running on approximately zero hours of sleep. And more than once, while both babies lay in their cribs crying into the air, I sat in the next room screaming into a pillow. I hated my life and every night, as a tear rolled down my cheek, I wondered, *Is this all there is in life?*

Why hadn't anyone warned me how mundane my days would be? I had gone to college full of excitement for the next chapter of life, but none of the courses I took prepared me for the mundane and unchallenging jobs that followed. Once the babies were born, my college degree seemed useless. I spent my days in a cycle of wash, dry, fold, feed, sleep, and repeat. Then there were the decisions that consumed my mind, decisions that weren't important but seemed crucial: What's for dinner? What should the babies and I wear? (I don't know why I ever worried about that because we would all be covered in some kind of bodily fluid shortly after getting dressed.) Which generic products were okay to buy, and which weren't? How should I organize the toys? Which coupons should I clip? Should I breastfeed, or is a bottle better? Do I really have to buy organic veggies? Is it really okay to have the babies immunized?

I lived in constant, overwhelming fear that I would make the wrong decision and ruin my family's health. I was paralyzed with anxiety, certain I was doing it all wrong. I needed a manual or, at the very least, some wisdom, so I sought help from a therapist. After I had confided in him about my guilt for feeling trapped in my life, he said, "Oh wow! I thought you were going to tell me you had an addiction to porn or something. This sounds pretty normal."

I wanted to scream.

Again.

I didn't want to be categorized as normal! I wanted to be the girl who used to jump off the bridge into the river, who dreamed of skydiving and traveling the world. Where was the girl who was spontaneous, adventurous, and fearless? Sure, I had dreamed of living the perfect, stay-at-home mom life, but I never imagined that it could come at the cost of losing myself. I loved my family, but I hated my normal, difficult, mediocre, blessed life. *What was wrong with me?*

Apparently, not enough. The therapist spent less than an hour with me before telling me I wasn't a candidate for his services. Just as we wrapped up the failed session, he offered this one bit of advice: "Before you make any decisions, I want you to ask yourself one question: *Am I doing this (or not doing this) because of fear, obligation, or guilt?* If the answer is *yes*, then make a different decision."

Whatever.

I left his office feeling defeated. As I drove home, I told myself to just accept my life for what it was: mediocre. Most people I knew lived *normal* lives and seemed content. Maybe that's why I had worked so hard to create a life that looked like everyone else's. A life that's ordinary was what I expected. Instead of listening to my own heart or seeking God's direction, I had forged ahead, making a million decisions that had built the walls of a life that now trapped me. Resigned to a prison of my own making, I told myself to get over the desire for something more. Joy was something reserved for the rich and free—and I was neither.

> "Before you make any decisions, I want you to ask yourself one question: Am I doing this (or not doing this) because of fear, obligation, or guilt? If the answer is yes, then make a different decision."

In the weeks and months that followed, my days all looked the same. I continued to add bricks to my prison until the walls began to collapse. The weight of debt it took to sustain a life that looked like the life of every other stay-at-home mother I knew was too much for our one-income family. The bills piled up until, one day, my husband, Rob, and I sat on the basement floor and discussed our reality: We were broke. My dream, as monotonous as it felt, was just too big. I needed to get a job.

As much as I hated my "normal" life, I hated the thought of going back to work and putting my children in daycare even more. If I had to make meaningless decisions all day long, I much preferred to do it from the comfort of my home while raising my own children, not in some drab cubicle while someone else played with my kids.

I considered my options. My first idea, which I tried and failed miserably, was taking care of children in my home. After a short trial, I quickly realized that was not the right profession for me. I have to be honest: If you were going to leave your kids with someone else for fifty hours per week, it probably shouldn't be with me. Listen, we all have strengths. Mine is not crafting with or feeding other people's children. I don't even like crafting with my own children. Plus, if we were going to make a dent in the mountain of debt we had amassed, I needed way more than the one or two part-time kids I was watching—in addition to my own.

Um, no thanks.

The search for a viable option continued. I shared my struggle with a group of friends online who offered a few ideas, most of which could easily be dismissed. *No, I can't make hairbows and sell them on Etsy.* (Remember what I said about crafting?) *No, I'm not interested in being a virtual assistant and managing someone else's fabulous life.* (I wanted to live my *own* fabulous life.) Then one woman suggested I check out a new direct-selling opportunity. She had recently been to one of those home-party businesses where you invite your friends to invite their friends to buy your stuff. She didn't sell it, but she assured me this company was one to check out. I was tempted to dismiss the idea as quickly as I had the others. There were a lot of reasons it would never work: I didn't know enough people. I had never sold anything like that before. I had never run my own business. And then I remembered the therapist's question from all those months before: "Am I doing this (or not doing this) out of fear, obligation, or guilt?"

Fear was the only real reason I wanted to say no to the opportunity. I was afraid I would fail, afraid I would look stupid, afraid that I could be wasting time on something that might be a scam. But fear wasn't a good reason to say no, so I stepped out in faith and made a different decision.

I said yes!

That one little yes changed everything for my family. I could tell you all about that business now—about how it helped our family go from broke to debt-free, how I've met so many amazing friends because of it, and how I am so glad I said yes to giving it a shot. (Just ask me sometime!) But that isn't what this book is about.

This book is about the simple question that has helped me create a dream life that I actually love—a life that is exciting and inspired and uniquely *me*—one decision at a time.

For so many years, my freedom and joy were buried under the weight of those three little words: fear, obligation, and guilt. It's no wonder that those words create the acronym FOG. Until that heavy blanket of fear, obligation, and guilt lifted, I wandered through life feeling lost and unhappy. When I began to intentionally clear away the FOG by making decisions that were true and right for me, I discovered that life didn't have to be normal or mediocre. It could be extraordinary.

As the FOG lifted from my life, my dream of being a mother shifted from a series of mundane and tedious tasks to a satisfying and exciting journey. I've rediscovered that courageous girl who dared to try new things. I've even found the courage to share this message with you.

Today, I ask myself that question with almost every decision I make. From what to wear, to what to eat, and, of course, the big stuff too! I also ask the hundreds of women I coach in business each year to consider the same question. And now it's your turn. Are you making your decisions based on fear, obligation, or guilt? If so, I hope you will start making different decisions. Because when you make decisions that lift the FOG from your life, you'll find freedom and the confidence to live *your* best life—the life that God has planned for you. And in *that* life, you'll discover that your dreams are little compared to what God has planned for you.

Your dreams are little compared to what God has planned for you.

Chapter 2

Liar, Liar

While my dad, stepmom, and half-brother lived in lovely Southern California, my older brother, Cleve, and I lived in Illinois with my mom in a simple black and white mobile home. Cleve and I went to stay with my dad in California every year for a month in the summer. The lavishness of those summer vacations and my mom's amazing budgeting skills kept my brother and me from realizing how poor we really were. We wore hand-me-down designer clothes that my mom got from friends at work (so we always looked great even if a year or two behind the current fashion). And due to the fact that my mom can stretch a dollar from Illinois to Timbuktu, I grew up thinking that when people talked about the American dream, *we* were living it.

By the time I was in second grade and Cleve was in fourth, we were staying home alone. My mom worked long days, so we let ourselves into the house and warmed up our own TV dinners. You know, the ones with the so-called mashed potatoes, gummy and stuck to the side of the paper tray and covered with brown gravy.

Salisbury steak was my favorite with the soggy excuse for fried chicken as a close second. My mom would come home at night exhausted, but she made sure we did our homework and there was always plenty to eat. Although life was simple and challenging, I felt loved inside our four walls.

I spent a lot of time playing with my cat and watching MTV as a kid. The MTV era was in full swing when I was in third grade, and I would watch those music videos and imagine what it would be like to be famous. Third grade doesn't seem like a milestone year, but it's the year I first became aware of everyone else—and that awareness made me feel more awkward than ever before. As I danced alone in front of the TV and sang into my hairbrush, I daydreamed about looking like my favorite pop stars and wearing clothes that made me feel pretty. Some fishnet lace, an off-the-shoulder sweatshirt, and some Converse tennis shoes would have changed my world!

At school, I overheard my teachers talking about the "cute" girls. I noticed that those girls all seemed to have freckles, so I used my mom's eyeliner pencil to draw some of my own. No one seemed to notice. I also noticed that none of the other girls at school wore mix and match hand-me-down clothes. Instead, they sported matching denim patchwork tops and bottoms and Keds (real ones, not the phony knock-offs from Woolworth's like the ones I wore). To my knowledge, no one realized I was wearing hand-me-downs. Still, I dreamed about going to the mall and picking out my very own outfits with matching hairbows. I wanted to be beautiful, but more than that, I wanted to be noticed. I wanted to be noticed so much that I begged my mom to let me get my long hair cut really short, just like Molly Ringwald, my favorite actress. To my surprise, she agreed, and it worked; I got a lot of attention. Unfortunately, it came in the form of name-calling. Apparently, I looked even less like a celebrity and more like a little boy. My plan backfired, and I became the laughing stock of the third grade.

When you live in a trailer park, you don't realize what everyone else says about the trailer park kids. All your friends live in a mobile home. They wear hand-me-down clothes and make their own TV dinners, just like you. You don't think about life outside your little community because it's all you know. But once you get invited to a birthday party at a house that isn't on wheels, things change. Now in the third grade, my haircut was enough to keep me from getting invited to any birthday parties outside the trailer park. But my brother did, and he told me all about the grassy backyards—complete with trampolines. It sounded like heaven!

Leslie and Karen were two of the prettiest girls in school. They had lots of freckles and lived in "real" houses. They talked a lot about all of the Care Bears and Cabbage Patch Dolls they had. I had a Cabbage Patch doll too. She was homemade, and I named her Nancy. (I never talked about Nancy in front of Leslie and Karen.) Those girls weren't mean to me, but they never invited me to slumber parties with them or to sit with them at lunch. Even though I had my own friends, I longed to fit in with the beautiful girls.

Then one day, in the school's lost-and-found display—a glass case we passed by every day on the way to gym class—I saw just the right thing to help me fit in: a beautiful headband. There, stuck on top of a paper mâché volcano (How does someone misplace a paper mâché volcano?) was the prettiest pink headband with a big white lace bow on top. And I wanted it! I knew it belonged to someone else, but I thought, *It's in the lost and found. It's not really stealing, is it? More like finders, keepers. That pretty headband should be on someone's head and not on that ugly volcano.*

Yep, I took that headband right off that volcano and slapped it on my head and thought, *No one will call me a boy now!* At least five people complimented me in the first hour. The kids may not have noticed that I wore hand-me-down jeans to school, but they sure noticed when I had something beautiful on top of my head. I loved the attention because it made me feel accepted.

That feeling was short lived, however. By hour two, the rightful owner of the headband, who happened to be Leslie, let me know that she lost a headband just like that yesterday. "Oh I'm sorry to hear that; it is the prettiest headband I've ever seen! I hope you find yours," I fibbed. Leslie was on to me. She immediately told her friends, who told my trailer park friends, who, it turns out, don't like liars either. I was busted.

Rather than admit I'd snagged it from the lost and found, I stuck to my lie—and added to it when Leslie and her posse of friends confronted me on the playground. I told them I had bought the headband with my mom and ,"no, this one didn't come with a shirt attached to it." Soon my hole was so deep that I had landed myself into the principal's office.

I think it's time we clear the air for the principals of the 1980s. There was no paddle in his office and no threats of spankings. But there was sternness and disappointment in his voice. I was mortified. All I had wanted was to be pretty and popular. Instead, taking that headband and fabricating a story about it had earned me the reputation of a liar and a thief. I longed to feel loved and accepted but was left feeling guilty and alone.

That was the first time I remember making a decision because I feared not being accepted. I felt obligated to impress my classmates. And in the end, I felt guilty for letting so many people down in my quest for affirmation. I wish that I could tell you that I learned my lesson at eight years old, but the truth is that I spent the next twenty years letting fear, obligation, and guilt rule my decisions.

Dear reader, I hope that you have stumbled across this book at the perfect time in your life, in a season where you are tired of making decisions out of fear, obligation, and guilt. You may not be stealing headbands, but you are likely robbing yourself of joy. Each time you do something out of fear, obligation, or guilt, you give away small pieces of yourself. What does it look like? Well, see if you can relate to any of the following:

> **Each time you do something out of fear, obligation, or guilt, you give away small pieces of yourself.**

- You answer the phone, even though the person on the other end doesn't treat you with respect and always leaves you feeling worse about yourself.
- You haven't had a girl's night out in ages because you are stretched thin with obligations and have no time for fun.
- You feel lonely, even in a room full of people, because no one really knows you.
- You are just so tired of not being able to keep up with everyone around you that you've decided to just let yourself go, never taking time for self-care.
- You question your worth and values because you feel you should be satisfied with your life, but you just aren't.
- You spend money you don't have so you can keep up appearances.
- No matter how hard you try to be happy for simple things like good friends, a healthy family, and a job that pays the bills most months, you just can't shake the feeling that there must be more to life.

I've been there. I've felt the exhaustion that comes from holding up the charade. I know how frustrating it can be when you're doing everything you can and getting nowhere, while everyone else seems to be taking strides towards success and joy. That exhaustion and frustration may be clues that you are not living the life God intends for you—your best life.

Before we get too far into this book, I need to be clear. I'm not saying that life can or should be all sunshine and roses all the time. Too much sun leads to sunburn, and even the most beautiful roses have thorns. Some days are hard—even when we are true to ourselves. (If you're under the illusion that my life is perfect, check my Instagram feed for a reality check!) What I am promising is that living under the weight of fear, doing things solely out of an obligation to meet others' expectations, or letting guilt guide your decisions will never lead you to

Some days are hard—even when we are true to ourselves.

the life you were created to live. And if you persist in living a lie (like I did with that stolen headband), you will never discover the true gifts God intended for you.

So what lies are you telling yourself or others? We all do it. Without considering the truth, we answer, "I'm fine," when someone asks how we're doing. We say yes when we really want to say no. We tell ourselves we "have to" do certain things and that we can't change our circumstances. Those lies hold us back. They make us feel guilt without cause. They push us to act out of obligation or fear rather than love or hopeful expectation.

You have a purpose—a life that God has designed specifically for you. Stepping into that life will require letting go of those lies. When you do, you'll begin to shine so brightly with purpose and passion, the FOG won't be able to stop you.

Chapter 3

Fear of Missing Out

*W*hen I was in high school, if there was an empty space in my week, I wanted it filled. In addition to maintaining decent grades and holding a part-time job, I participated in art club, cheerleading, track, school musicals, yearbook, and I was on the student council. (And that was just in the spring semester!) I wanted to experience all life had to offer.

That desire never really went away.

As a kid, I was called a "joiner" or a "social butterfly," and that pattern continued in college. In fact, when I was a college freshman, one of my professors asked me if I knew the difference between being lonely and being alone. At the time, I thought the words were synonymous. I worked hard at never being alone, yet I felt completely lonely.

When my children started preschool and I began working from home, I never said no to an invitation—*come to my party, plan a raffle for the school, join our volunteer opportunity, come to this women's retreat, come to this learning event, there's a new fitness class*. I went to everything and lived by the rule, *always be one of the last to leave*. After all, you never know when something great might happen at the PTO meeting (said no one ever).

People would compliment me, as if being involved in *everything* was an achievement. They would say, "You're so good at balancing everything," or "Is there anything you can't do?" Trust me, I was no good at balancing; it was all smoke and mirrors. I was constantly forgetting things, running late, yelling at my husband, and cussing at the dog on the way out the door. It was a toss-up as to whether a four-letter word or flood of tears would escape first. I was exhausted and missing out on what meant the most to me: quality family time, time for me to read or be creative, and intimacy with my husband.

> I was exhausted and missing out on what meant the most to me: quality family time, time for me to read or be creative, and intimacy with my husband.

In all my efforts to be involved, I gave up time with the people who are most important to me. It's not that all those things and people I spent time with were bad; they just weren't what really mattered to me. When I counted my blessings at the end of the day, those groups, parties, and meetings never ended up on my list.

Modern technology enabled me to be involved—even when I wasn't. When smartphones and social media first came on the scene, I would immediately respond to every post, email, or text. That magical *ding* had me running to check my phone for the latest update. (Seriously, the only thing I ever reacted to more quickly than my phone was hearing my firstborn make a choking sound after he spit up. Suddenly, I'd turn into a superhero running to save the day. Never mind that I didn't know anything about CPR.

Inevitably, by the time I got to him, that sweet boy had a little grin on his face. Now that I think about it, that sound could have been his way of testing how quickly he could get my attention.)

I was constantly connected, but I never slowed long enough for real connection.

Do you know that feeling of disconnection and loneliness in the middle of a crowd? Have you let go of something in your life that you used to love dearly? Is that "thing" sitting right in front of you (like your husband), waiting for you to show love and positive attention—instead of a constant nagging or disapproval? Are you so wrapped up in looking perfect or busy that you have forgotten how to just be in the moment and connect? I know that feeling.

Even in the middle of all that busyness, I would ask myself why I was sacrificing my time and money to serve, socialize, and impress other people. But without thinking too much about the reason, I continued to stretch myself thin, going and joining, planning and committing. I felt as if I were running on a hamster wheel. I convinced myself that slowing down would mean letting people down. The thought of someone being disappointed in me was much more frightening than my next meltdown on the way to a playdate.

I convinced myself that slowing down would mean letting people down.

"What is wrong with me?" I wondered. Did other women feel similar pressure to be everything to everyone? When I least expected it, I found validation in a conversation with a friend. As I shared my busy season of life with her, she said "Oh, you have FOMO!" My first thought was, *What did you call me?* She explained that FOMO meant *fear of missing out.* "My teen daughter says it all the time."

The fact that someone, somewhere, named my inability to miss out on pretty much anything was proof that there were others just like me. I thought, *I should form a support group.* But then I realized that anyone who joined would only come for fear they may miss out on something if they didn't.

I soon discovered that many people suffer from FOMO to some extent. If I were a betting woman, I would bet you have FOMO too. The last time you left your phone at home when you went to the grocery store, did you turn the car around right away to go get it? If so, you have pretty severe FOMO. If you continued on your journey phoneless but reached into your purse anyway to grab your phone and check for notifications, welcome to the FOMO club. Yes, you have it too.

Perhaps because we have constant access to our smartphones, we have become obsessed with immediate notifications. Do you grab your phone first thing in the morning to see what you missed while you were sleeping? Do you check Facebook while you are at a stoplight (or even *while* you are driving)? ABC News reported that the average American checks their smartphone 150 times per day! That means with only six hours of sleep, Americans are still checking smartphones one time every seven minutes.[1]

FOMO is about way more than phone notifications, though. And it's not always about going to parties or meeting fun new people. For me, it was about *the news.* No, not the local TV news that comes on at 6:00 and 10:00 each night. I was addicted to the news about my friends (however distant or loosely acquainted we were), when it involved marriage, babies, job changes, promotions, new houses, vacations—you name it! I never wanted to miss out on a great recipe, a cute craft, a great decorating solution, a party idea, or anything else the world of social media deemed important. I couldn't *not* comment on how to hard boil an egg correctly or wrap a sprained ankle (even though I likely would have to do a little Google research first).

I wanted to soak up every bit of data possible. The more I knew about others' lives, the more confidence I felt about my own. I longed for people to rely on me for the latest scoop on my friends and acquaintances. It made me feel more important, needed, even worthy when people took my advice. And it felt good to have a wide circle of friends—even if most of them were people I had never actually met.

Sure, I sought positive ammo to fuel my fire for knowledge, but I overindulged to the point that staying connected and "in the know" disrupted my sleep and consumed my thoughts. I felt that my work was done for the day only when that red notification bubble had disappeared.

My constant involvement in social media conversations made me feel significant. It wasn't that I believed that gracing people with my presence, my advice, or my witty comments would make their day. It was quite the opposite. I attempted to fill my own cup with the fallacy that if I showed up to everything, eventually someone would *really* need me. My fear of missing out was a quest to find wholeness and value in my own life. And in the process of seeking that kind of significance, my real-life and spiritual well-being connections suffered. I didn't look to my family to fill my need for love and importance; in fact, I acted as though I were too busy answering the questions of my virtual family to engage with my reality family. Instead of seeking out biblical truths to understand my worth, I tried to find my value in the virtual world. But "virtual love" can never fill the longing we all have to be truly loved by our Creator. As hard as I tried to never miss a post, comment, or Kodak moment, I could never get my fill of information, value, or love.

I would watch my children stop to smell flowers, raise their arms out to their sides when a gentle breeze blew their hair, feel raindrops fall on their face, or taste snowflakes on their tongues. They would stop every time, even if we passed that same flower ten times a day. This time, just like all the others, my youngest daughter wanted to stop and smell the nicely potted flowers outside the library. Annoyed, I commanded her to keep moving. Bewildered by my flustered tone, she looked at me and said, "Why do we have to hurry, Momma? I thought we didn't have any plans today."

There I stood speechless (which is not my natural state). I realized that in my rush to mark one more thing off my list, I was teaching my children that the intricacies of God's creation aren't worth our wonder. My kids rarely missed the beauty of God's gifts on any given day, but my thirst to not miss anything had me missing everything that was beautiful. And then, in times of hardships, I would wonder, *Where is God? Why hasn't He shown His face to me lately?* All the time, He was surrounding me with displays of His love and grace—I just never took the time to notice. I wondered how many beautiful details, how many precious moments with my family, I had missed. My daughter's question that day shook me into a new awareness.

I suddenly realized that each time I said yes to anything, I was saying no to something else. I found myself staying up late at night, surfing through the social media channels of everyone else's life, when I should have, in fact, been engaging in my own. I began to wonder how many rich, life-changing conversations I missed because I was thinking about moving onto the next person, post, or activity? I would be dialed into my screen but hear laughter in the background and feel sadness because I had missed whatever was causing such joy. I was certain nothing on the screen was causing me joy. In fact, it was the opposite. I noticed the more I engaged the screen, the more I needed it. Like a moth to a flame, my tasks and screens would draw me in. I was concerned with checking off the next box and not concerned enough with the people whom the checked box represented. Instead of slowing down long enough to make one person in a room feel seen, loved, and connected, I was making ten people feel *kind of* important or, worse yet, completely ignored.

Prior to that day with my daughter, I hurried through dissatisfying prayer and devotional times—with my phone in hand. Or I simply slept in, leaving no time for connection with God. Suddenly, I realized that with all my rushing around, I had neglected the relationship that matters most. Now I knew the Lord was calling me to be still, and I listened because now I feared missing out on the messages He had for me. God tells me that I am wonderfully made (Psalm 139:14), and I am precious and honored (Isaiah 43:4). Although I had seen these words before, I had never made the time to rest on them, to fully allow them to settle into my heart.

> I realized that with all my rushing around, I had neglected the relationship that matters most.

By creating margins for stillness, I was finally able to see how much FOMO had cost me.

How many times had I promised my children a game of Go Fish that I never got to because I *needed* to respond to this "real quick" text that turned into a fifteen-minute conversation?

- How often had I told my son I wouldn't sit down and color with him because I was busy cleaning up the dishes?
- When did I mindlessly answer "mmm-hmmm" to my husband when he told me about his day because I was busy creating tomorrow's to-do list?

- How often had I told a friend we should get together for coffee sometime but never followed through, convincing myself I didn't have time for coffee, all the while spending hours connected virtually to people I hardly knew?

All of these little demands that continue to grab at my attention are not from my Creator but from the great distractor. The enemy knows that if he can keep you and me distracted by the little things, the big things will slip right past us. Convicted by my daughter's innocence and wonder, I determined to focus my attention on the beauty God placed in my path each day—including my family. Fighting FOMO took conscious effort. And in this battle, I stopped and hunted for frogs with my seven-year-old son. I stopped and smelled the flowers with my daughter, even if we smelled the same ones yesterday. We wondered together in amazement at the details God has made in *all* of creation. I'm so glad I didn't miss those moments.

I began to say no or at least, "Let me think about it," rather than automatically accepting every invitation or request on my time. As my calendar cleared, my heart lightened, and I felt less stressed. The relief showed up in subtle, and sometimes silly, ways—like when I laughed from my gut when someone let out some surprise gas at the dinner table. No longer stretched to the point of breaking, I could see humor in the little things and enjoy being present in the moment.

It has taken time—and it still requires intention—but I can honestly say that today, I am present. I am here, in *this* moment. The task list can wait. Facebook can wait. And the notifications are turned *off* on my phone. Today, I don't worry about missing out on what's next. My fear is of missing out on the moments that will create lasting memories for my family.

Join the Fight against FOMO

My fight against FOMO began the day my daughter questioned my inexplicable need to rush. But the war wasn't won in a day. It has taken time and repeated refocusing of my attention to get to the point where I live in the here and now. Don't underestimate the battle with FOMO. It's an addiction that takes one day at a time to overcome.

The best way to conquer FOMO is to simply start missing out. Similar to working a muscle, the more often you train that muscle, the stronger it will get. Put your phone in the other room, don't go to the meeting, or leave the party early. Try leaving the dishes in the sink at bedtime or the toys on the floor all the way through naptime—and use the time you gain to indulge in something you love doing. The super exciting part is finding you haven't missed out on anything, and soon you will have more energy to focus on what is most important, like rest, downtime with your family, and maybe even sex again—like the kind where you aren't distracted by all the little things.

> Don't underestimate the battle with FOMO. It's an addiction that takes one day at a time to overcome.

I know you might be thinking, *If I don't sign up to be the coach this year, there won't be a soccer team.* You might be right. Maybe this year there will not be a soccer team. In that case, there will be some disappointed children who will either find another soccer team where you aren't the coach, find another activity for this season, or maybe (hopefully) their parents will follow your lead and enjoy a more relaxed season. Maybe next season another parent will step forward, or maybe by then your child will have moved onto something new. That's okay! Because unless you're raising a professional soccer player (and my guess is that you're not), missing a season of soccer isn't going to hurt your child's chances for success in life.

I want to encourage you to think about every demand or request for your time in light of the greater scheme of life. If an activity won't be important in five or ten years, it probably shouldn't consume us *now*. Think about this: Is it more important to your child's future and well-being that you are the soccer coach (or troop leader or cheer coach or whatever) or that you are a present mother and wife? Do you want your legacy to be one of busyness and anxiety or one of peace and prayer? Because you cannot have both. No matter how much others tell you that you rock at balancing it all, your children, your husband, and your family see through your act, and they will miss you.

If FOMO has been ruling your time and distracting you from what really matters, I hope you'll join me in the battle. What will you say no to *today*? How will you show up *today*? Remember, it takes one day at a time to overcome this addiction, and it starts when you decide to be present in your life and in the lives of those you love. In Chapter 10, we will

What will you say no to *today*?

take a closer look at your obligations and sort out how to identify your real opportunities to shine. We will identify what you are called to do versus what you are capable of doing, and I will even teach you *how* to say no without the guilt. But for right now, let's start with one simple habit that can get your day started with the right focus.

Instead of grabbing your phone first thing in the morning to check your Instagram feed, spend time journaling, praying, or listening to an inspirational podcast. Use the first minutes of your day to bring *your* goals and values into focus—rather than allowing yourself to be distracted by what everyone else is doing. Create a cozy spot in your home with a comfortable place to sit, complete with fun pillows, a cozy blanket, and a little stool or table where you can prop your feet. It's important that this space feels *good* to you and that it's quiet. Next, buy a cute journal. Do not go on using the one subject notebook from the kids' leftover school supplies. When your corner is cozy and your notebook is chic, you'll show up to your happy space ready to relax, spend time with God, and focus on yourself.

It's so easy to skip this quiet time in the morning. You may even be thinking, *I don't have time to just sit around!* You do; you're just spending it doing something else. And if you don't have fifteen spare minutes in your day, you must reexamine your schedule—which is easy enough when you decide not to check your phone first thing in the morning. Since we are replacing your old FOMO with new, healthier habits, this quiet time is the perfect replacement for one of your mindless social media appointments. Plus, the God who created the universe deserves at least fifteen minutes of your time, since He is the reason you woke up breathing today! You may have to stop pushing snooze each morning, but I promise that those fifteen minutes of sleep were not going to fill your spirit like these moments of prayer and journaling. And I have found that this quiet time actually makes me more productive in the areas that mean the most.

The physical release of your words out of your mind and onto paper is therapeutic. Think of it like this: When you get your oil changed in your car, the bad oil needs to be emptied before the fresh oil can be added. When you start your day, your worries and fears can be emptied on paper in the form of prayers. Jotting down worries, confessions, and fears then leaving them for God to handle will clear your heart for the goodness and meaning that will be poured into your life as you make time to see God all around you.

The journal isn't for others to read, so if necessary, put it somewhere safe so you can write freely, and then make sure you do. I love writing my prayers because it's fun to look back occasionally and see the work that God has done. There will be days you feel like writing pages and days you only feel like writing a few sentences. This is your time with God, so there are no rules, and you don't need to hide anything from Him, not on paper nor in your heart. If writing your prayers out feels too personal and scary, try starting with a list of worries or fears, then finish with an equal number of things that cause you to feel gratitude.

Once you get that dirty oil out of your engine, replenish it with the truths God says about you. You don't even need to go to the bookstore. A few resources that I have really enjoyed are the daily emails from Proverbs 31 Ministries and Holley Gerth's book, *You're Already Amazing*. And, of course, there is always *the* source: the Bible. Consider getting a *Life Application Study Bible*, as it walks you through how to use Scripture and apply it to your daily life. If you are like me, sometimes all of those "thees" and "thous" can get a little overwhelming. A Life Application Study Bible breaks down the Scriptures into understandable language without compromising the integrity of the message. The goal is to find bite-sized teaching that can fill your heart with truth.

There are mornings when I am so exhausted and don't want to write in my journal, or I have nothing to say (trust me, that's rare). But on those mornings, I wake up, drag myself to my cozy space, and say to Him, "I'm here, God! Hold me and just keep doing what you're doing." Just listen to your heartbeat, listen to the messages that repeat over and over. This is how God speaks to you. During these quiet ticks of the clock, your decision to conquer your fear of missing out on earthly commitments will be solidified. Peace will replace your fear, and you'll continue creating space for what gives your life true meaning and purpose.

Chapter 4

The Great Comeback

There is a myth in the direct-selling industry that people who start with a brand-new company are more likely to succeed. The buzz phrase "ground-floor opportunity" creates a swarm of interest with new enrollees. I started as an independent consultant with Thirty-One—a direct-selling company that offers personalized bags, organizational accessories, and other gifts—when the company was only four years old. I had never been part of the direct-selling industry before, so it didn't occur to me to consider how young the company was or whether it was a "ground-floor opportunity." I just saw some products that I really liked and a way for me to stay home with my kids, so I jumped at the opportunity.

I've worked hard to build my business. So it bothered me (a lot) that the common response I heard from people after they learned that my team consists of thousands of consultants was, "Well, good for you! You must have gotten in at the right time." For years, I felt a tremendous desire to defend my success and tell those people exactly how hard I had to work to get to the top level of leadership—and still work to stay there. You see, success in this business has very little to do with when you start; the determining factor for success is persistence. I'm successful because I spent many late nights training my team, showed up consistently, and held successful parties—even after holding parties that were complete flops that made me want to quit. I built strong relationships, which takes time away from my family. I managed friendships over hard business decisions, which takes hours of prayer and unfaltering faith. I've put in the time, effort, sweat, and tears to grow a successful business; luck or starting "at the right time" had nothing to do with it. It was the thousands of tiny decisions and years of consistent action that led me to being one of the very first National Executive Directors for the company.

Perhaps the reason that "right time" comment struck a nerve with me for so long was that I wondered if there was some truth behind it. Would my hard work not have paid off if I started three years later? In moments of frustration, that little voice of self-doubt piped up: *Maybe I'm not really that smart—just lucky.*

For nine years, I pushed down those thoughts and redirected myself to the truth: I had worked hard, and I knew for sure that God directed me to this career after a desperate prayer to live a life free of fear, obligation, and guilt.

But then a company-wide announcement rocked my confidence and distracted me from focusing on the truth. The career path I had conquered was being restructured. At first, I welcomed the announcement. I knew our company needed to make changes in order to ensure long-term growth and stability. I was confident that the changes being made would keep the company, my team, and, thus, my income strong for years to come. I welcomed the changes because they didn't really affect me. I was safe, performing well above the standards. Sure, I felt bad for the people it would affect with lower commissions, but I wasn't worried for myself or my income.

This restructure took about eighteen months to take full effect.

You know why they say not to count your chickens before they hatch? Because things change, and eggs are not chickens. I was overly confident and didn't protect my eggs during this long transition period. I went from feeling secure with my title and income level to having only half of what I needed to maintain what I had built. When the final transition took place, I was demoted, defeated, and embarrassed.

My first response was blame. I quickly started with an "if" list—and it didn't include me:

- If the company had . . .
- If my team were . . .
- If my customers liked . . .
- If my family wasn't . . .

The list of ifs and blames went on. The comment that had bugged me for years now seemed true. My mind ran wild with doubts: *Maybe it wasn't my abilities that helped me get to the top. Maybe I truly had been in the right place at the right time, and now here I am watching the bottom fall out. All these years, people have been laughing behind my back, poking fun at my belief in what I was doing. Maybe they were right!*

I had spent years defending myself. I had believed in the company and had trusted God for His direction. Faced with a lower title and lower pay, I wondered if I had been a fool. *Did God really deliver me this gift just to take it all away? Am I really just a girl from the trailer park who was in the right place at the right time? Would I ever be good enough to be a true success?*

When the "ifs" and blame had run their course, I was exhausted. But I wasn't ready to quit. I picked myself up off the floor (where I'd spent far too much time crying, excuse-making, and perhaps not enough praying) and considered which of the "if's" I could influence. Maybe *if* instead of complaining to God, I would actually stop and listen for His direction, I would find that He had been guiding me all along. *If* God says nothing can separate me from Him (Romans 8:35–39), I am His child (John 1:12, Galatians 3:26), I was made perfect in His creation (Genesis 1:31), I find peace and joy in His presence (Philippians 4:6–9), then why was I feeling distracted, deceived, and defeated? What if none of the fear and failings I was facing were God's doing, but rather Satan's efforts to manipulate me into thinking they were?

In Genesis, Eve, the mother of all creation, was the first to question God's intentions. His instructions were pretty simple: You get it all, the whole entire Garden of Eden, just don't eat the fruit from that one tree. The serpent slithered up to Eve and planted the seeds of doubt: "Did God actually say you couldn't eat that? Because when you do, you will know good *and* evil" (Genesis 3:1, 5, paraphrased). His statement implies that prior to the bite of fruit, she only knew good. Everything in her life was good.

No matter how many times I read this story, I find myself mentally screaming (not unlike the way my husband yells at the TV during a football game), "Don't do it, Eve! STOP! Stay focused." Yet every time, the outcome is the same. Eve, distracted and manipulated, loses sight of what she knows is true. She goes from living a life with zero shame, no remorse, no regret—just pure peace and contentment—to hiding in shame and embarrassment from God.

I can't help but wonder what Eve was really thinking in the moment of her decision to eat that forbidden fruit. Was she fearful that without the full knowledge of everything within her reach, she wouldn't be enough? Did she long to control her environment so much that she was willing to sacrifice what she knew in her heart to be true, just for a taste of control? I can so relate to Eve. Maybe you can too. We both had so much—and longed for more. We both felt discontented despite being overwhelmingly blessed.

During the time I spent running that "if" list, I couldn't see that, even though I had been demoted, I was still running a very successful business, touching literally thousands of women's lives. I still had a job with the kind of flexibility and reward that most people could only dream of. My happiness was blinded by my desire for the highest title and the biggest income. I felt out of control, so I bathed in my disappointment and blame.

It took time, prayer, and good friends to pull me out of that pit of despair. This season of life was proof that good friends aren't always nice enough to dance in the pit of despair with you, but rather are tough enough to pull you out. It was that tough love that reminded me, no matter what my title or income, no one could take away what I had accomplished. Just like an Olympian is always an Olympian and a mother is always a mother, I determined to honor the accomplishment I had achieved—even if I wasn't capable of maintaining it.

What Will You Do When You Fail?

Where was your glorious moment and great stumble? Did you lose some weight and then gain it back? Were you once debt free but got caught in a bind that has buried you in debt again? Have you lost your passion to be a great mother and wife, even though you remember a time when it was something you were passionate about? You did it once; you can own that. More importantly, if you did it once, you can do it again—or you can do something even greater. Sometimes we don't go back to where we were; sometimes we find a new, better place. Or we may find a place that is equally good but with a new perspective of gratitude we didn't have before the failure. What might God be teaching you during your comeback? This time, maybe you'll recognize God's purpose in the journey. Is it possible that you need to accomplish this mission twice to really trust yourself and embrace the power you own?

We all fail at some point, which means we are all faced with the choice to get back up or to stay in that pit of shame, overwhelmed with guilt and fearful of trying only to fail again. If you're stuck in that pit now, let me be the friend who encourages you to climb out. Start by thinking about what it is that you want to achieve—and why you want to achieve it. Take some time to think not about why you want this goal but rather what it will look like when you have accomplished it. How will you feel when you look back at the work you did and say, "WOW! I did that!" With your goal and your wow moment clear in your mind, identify three action steps you can take right away that will move you closer to your goal.

For myself, my goal was to regain my title and rebuild my income. To do that, I needed to identify where things had gone wrong. I began by asking the people in my organization to help me identify some areas I lacked. It was tough to ask these questions. "Please point out where I am failing." The thought even now makes me cringe. The key to accepting the answers of these hard questions is to remember that the truth lies somewhere between the harshest comment and the most uplifting one. Next, I looked at the facts. Even though it was painful, I had to look at the numbers to see where there was room for the most improvement. Just like in weight loss, when you have to step on the scale, or in budgeting, when you have to look at the current spending habits on paper, I had to look to see what numbers I had control over.

None of these steps were easy. Have you ever gone to the doctor's office, stepped on the scale, then looked the opposite direction so you didn't have to see the number? It doesn't change the number if you don't look. The facts are the facts; the sooner you face them, the sooner you can find resources to help you move to a number you want to see. For me, I found that going back to the basics of my business was the best place to start. I had made things too complicated and gotten so exhausted by the things distracting me from the truth. I needed to only focus on building relationships and finding out how I could most impact someone's life. Was it by the perfect gift, the opportunity to have a fun girls' night, or by helping them learn to make additional income for their family? If I were on a weight loss journey, I would look at how much and what I'm eating, as well as how much I am moving. The basics never fail, but they can often get crowded out by the distractions. So what is it for you? What is the first thing you need to do to get yourself back on track? One step at a time; you can do this! Your big comeback is on the horizon!

What is the first thing you need to do to get yourself back on track?

Here's the amazing truth: The comeback is always more inspiring and triumphant than the setback. The proof is in Jesus. If Eve had never sinned, the fall that cursed humankind might never have occurred. Believers would have never fully experienced the love and sacrifice that God displayed by sending Jesus to the cross. Sure, it's cool to think about the world that was perfect and serene. But what's more moving is thinking about how broken it all was, and still is, and that God loved us so much that He sent Jesus to die for us. The comeback is so much more celebrated than the original. We don't have a holiday that celebrates the world in its perfection before the fall, but we *do* have a holiday to celebrate the comeback, the saving of our world, the grace that surrounds us all after we hid from sin and shame. Easter signifies that even though our world stumbled and fell hard, Jesus came and delivered the greatest comeback of all time by defeating death.

What does Jesus's resurrection—the most amazing comeback of all time—have to do with you? Well, my sweet friend, I find that most women have the same fears that Eve had so long ago. Eve first feared that she wasn't enough without just one more thing. When trying to find success in jobs, marriage, parenting, or physical health, women often believe they aren't enough. It's common for women to worry about a lack of resources or wrestle with a lack of self-confidence of belief when it comes to their ability to accomplish their vision. Or they may not dare to admit they even have a dream.

Daring to acknowledge and pursue your dream takes courage and tenacity, traits that can be hidden by fear, obligation, and guilt. Sometimes the FOG gets so thick, you may forget you ever possessed those traits at all.

But you do. You are braver and more capable than you may dare imagine.

If, or rather when, you are tempted to give up on your dream, return to that moment where you picture your job well done, that "wow" moment where you are so proud of what you have accomplished. Imagine what your life will be like when that dream becomes a reality. How will you feel? Who else will be positively affected? Push the FOG away and, for a moment, picture how you will celebrate your comeback.

See it? Feel it?

Good.

Now go after it, my friend. You've got this!

Chapter 5

What Successful Women Do Differently

I wave the white flag.
I surrender. I give up.
I'm abandoning ship.
I'm hanging it up.

How many times have you just wanted to quit? You feel as if you've given "it" (whatever it is) everything you've got. The logical next step is to walk away before matters get worse.

Or is it?

If you do quit, is there a possibility that you'd be walking away before matters get better?

You may know that Michael Jordan, known for over a decade to be the world's best basketball player, was cut from his high school basketball team. It is also thought that Thomas Edison tried 1,000 times to invent the light bulb before it actually worked. Although no real source was documented, it is widely believed that when asked how it felt to fail 1,000 times while making the light bulb, Edison's reply was, "I didn't fail 1,000 times. The light bulb was an invention with 1,000 steps."[1]

When it comes to success and failure, being persistent and having the right perspective is everything. What if Michael Jordan had never gone back the next year for basketball tryouts? What if Thomas Edison stopped trying to invent on try number 998? What if you are one month, one step, one decision away from the greatest moment of your life?

Get Back Up (Again)

If you think about it, the greatest successes are built on beautiful stories of failure—sometimes *repeated* failure. From the outside looking in, we don't always see the defeat the people in those success stories had to overcome along the way. What we see is how easy life looks for them. We think, *Wow! It must be nice to be that smart, gifted, talented, lucky, blessed, and loved* (insert whatever word you admire and envy in someone). The reality is, behind every success story is a saga of hard work, sleepless nights, injuries, and failed attempts.

We watch the Olympics and see an elegant skater fall and get right back up, and we wonder, *How did she just get up and act as if that didn't happen?* She has the ability to get back up because she's fallen down and gotten up a million times before. That's why it all looks so easy, even the part where she failed and tried again. Does that mean she is smarter than you? More gifted than you? No. It means that she is conditioned to believe in herself, even if she fails. She is disciplined enough not to sit and cry but rather get up and try again. No one says that getting up after falling down isn't hard, but it is necessary.

Dating after divorce or the tragic loss of a spouse, going back to school after all these years, taking a leap of faith to start a new business when the last one failed, trying for a child after the loss of a pregnancy, or getting your body back into shape after years of letting it go. I get it. It's not just hard; it's really hard. Sometimes the fear is paralyzing. The pain of loss or embarrassment that could come from losing (again) seems like more than you can bear. That fear is like a prison where the desires of our hearts stay locked away, as if we are safer with them hidden in the dark corner of our heart than out in the open where they are exposed to risk and ridicule. It's only by unlocking that prison door, however, that true success is possible.

After more than a decade of coaching women to succeed in business, I have noticed that those who attain the greatest success share three things in common. The first is that, like the Olympian, Michael Jordan, and Thomas Edison, they practice persistence. They refuse to give up. They view each obstacle they stumble upon as a chance to learn something new—even if that means finding a new path. Every decision is either a blessing or a lesson. But no obstacle can make these successful women quit.

Don't Go It Alone

The second trait successful women possess is that they don't journey alone. They always have someone by their side to support and guide them—and they help others along the way. Because we are all human. We will have days that are difficult or seem downright impossible. That's when being accountable to someone we admire can nudge us to show up even when we don't want to. When successful women do stumble or feel lost, they seek help from someone who will cheer them on or help them get back up again.

Sometimes that person is their spouse, but more often than not, it's a friend or mentor they can turn to for advice and encouragement.

Busting the "Unsupportive Spouse/Friend/Parent" Excuses

If you're married, you might expect your husband to be your greatest supporter in every venture. If that's true for you, great! But if your spouse is unsupportive, you are not alone. Your closest friends, family members, and even your death-til-we-part partner in life may try to discourage you from following a big dream. They may see your dream as a risky business venture. They may doubt that you'll succeed in a health journey, especially if you have tried before and failed.

Be careful not to use an unsupportive loved one as an excuse to give up (or never start) on your dream. That lack of support is simply an obstacle. (And remember, successful women find a way over, through, or around obstacles.) As long as you aren't putting your family through a major financial hardship or a risk of tragedy, you may have to look elsewhere for the guidance you need.

Get it out of your head that if your spouse/parent/best friend doesn't come alongside your journey, no one will. Lack of support from those closest to you is a cue to dig deep, uncover, respond to their main concerns, and perhaps even reevaluate your vision or methods. Is it you they doubt, or is it the industry, the principle, or the plan? Is it really that you cannot lose weight and they don't believe in your resolve to commit, or are you trying to take a shortcut, like a diet pill? If their concerns are legitimate and you properly address them, they may come around. If they refuse to come alongside you even after you've addressed any real concerns or misconceptions, find another supporter!

Your best supporter might be a mentor or someone who is just a bit further along the road you're taking. Seek out someone who has some life experience, who will cheer you on, and who will remind you of your wow moment when you feel like giving up.

As you lose the weight, earn the paycheck, or make progress toward whatever goal you were previously afraid to achieve, your spouse/friend/parent may turn into your biggest fan. (If they don't, you'll want to take note of the chapter on setting boundaries in toxic relationships.)

Just Ask!

The third attribute all successful women possess is that they ask for what they want. In our society, discrepancies still exist between what is socially acceptable for a man versus a woman when it comes to how we work and pursue our goals. If a man asks for what he wants and makes quick decisions, he is viewed as being strong and in charge. When a woman is decisive and assertive enough to ask for what she wants, she is sometimes labeled as overbearing or pushy.

I work in a sales industry. The truth is, I know some people avoid me because they assume I might be pushy. But I know I'm not pushy. The reason I know is because I have seen pushy, and pushy doesn't work. Pushy is when you ask for something and *insist* that the other person says yes, even if doing so puts that person in a bind. Pushy is really good for you and only you. So how do you know for sure if you are being too assertive? Stop and ask yourself: Is the request selfish, and is the other person free to say no? If your request comes out of a desire to advance without regard to other needs, you need to check your motives. But if you're like most women I know, your desire is to improve the world around you, not to push your ideals and selfish motives on it.

My dear friend, how often are you burying your real questions because you are worried that your requests will make you appear high maintenance or too assertive? Have you been keeping your wants, needs, and desires tucked into that dark corner, hiding your talents and gifts because you don't want to seem pushy? I'm not a feminist, but I do believe there are some cultural norms that could use some updating, and this is one of them. From this moment forward, let's start asking for exactly what we want or need.

What if you began to reach out today with direct questions and statements of intention?

I have always wanted to own my own business. Can you teach me how?

I would love to learn to play the piano. Do you know someone who teaches adults?

I think I'd like to adopt. Can we go talk to someone together?

I'd like to lose weight and feel better about myself. What services does your gym offer to help me achieve my goal?

Does it take big courage to state exactly what you want and to ask these questions? Absolutely! It can be hard to drum up that courage. But you know what else is hard? Living with regrets and unfulfilled dreams. It's hard getting up every morning and going to a job that builds someone else's dream and not your own. It's hard living as a divorcée, wading through weekends alone while your children are with their dad. It's hard to watch your friends having babies when you want nothing more than a child in your arms. And it's hard to be overweight, tired, and uncomfortable in your own skin. The beauty of life, especially in the United States, is that you have the freedom to choose which hard road you want to take.

Let's ask without the softeners of "let me know" or "I just wanted to check." Let's ask boldly! Stop saying "let me know" and start saying what you mean. "Let me know when you can meet for coffee" isn't the same as "I think I'd enjoy some company. Would you like to grab coffee with me tomorrow?" It is direct; it leaves no room for misinterpretation. Sure, it may leave you feeling raw and vulnerable. But as my junior-high-aged daughter pointed out, even if it feels uncomfortable to ask a question, at least you'll have an answer. We were chatting not long ago when she said, "Mom, I don't understand why you would even have a crush without telling them about it. I mean, if they don't know you have a crush, you'll always wonder if they liked you back." Well played, junior high, well played. I am not sure I'm ready for her to have crushes just yet, but I like the principle and the courage behind her thinking. I think that in adult terms I would say this: If you don't share how you feel and ask the hard questions, you'll never know what's possible. If you ask and the answer is no, nothing changes. But if you ask and the answer is yes, everything could change.

> If you ask and the answer is no, nothing changes. But if you ask and the answer is yes, everything could change.

In 1 Chronicles 4:10 (NIV), we read that "Jabez cried out to the God of Israel, 'Oh, that you would bless me and enlarge my territory! Let your hand be with me, and keep me from harm so that I will be free from pain.' And God granted his request." Jabez wasn't afraid to ask God for a big blessing. He could have said, "Dear Lord, please give me a little bit more," but instead he went big. He asked God to bless him abundantly, and what does that last sentence say? "God granted his request." *The Prayer of Jabez* by Bruce Wilkinson is one of my favorite short books. Wilkinson goes into depth about how using the tactic Jabez used, boldly asking God for what you want so He will bless you abundantly, is how we break through to a blessed life. Ask and you shall receive (Matthew 7:7). That doesn't mean that God is a genie granting your every wish. It does mean He wants you to come to Him and boldly ask for what you want. He loves to see you joyous and thriving, as long as you recognize that your hands alone could not have accomplished what He has accomplished through you.

A while back, one of my kids came to me and asked, "Mom, can I have an apple?"

"Of course, honey," I said.

A few minutes later, kid number two came to me and asked, "Mom, can I have a cookie?"

"Sure," I said.

Suddenly, kid number one was all ticked off *at me*, when I had done nothing wrong. If kid number one would have asked for a cookie, I would have said yes. Instead, she ended up crying all over her apple slices because "it isn't fair" that kid number two asked for what she wanted and got it.

Go get 'em, girlfriend!

The point of this little story is to ask for what you want. Exactly what you want. Not just what you think will be an easy yes. At the end of the day, if you don't get what you asked for, you haven't lost any ground; you've just gained an opportunity to share how your journey to success started with failure.

Chapter 6
Take Off the Mask

I'm going to start this chapter with a word of warning for my mom and mother-in-law: You may want to skip to the next chapter because I'm about ready to share my most embarrassing moment. While the rest of the world may think it's hilarious, you two may find the story . . . less than amusing.

When I was pregnant with my youngest child, I started listening to a podcast about healthy sexual relationships in marriage. Some of the things I heard really hit home because I was ready to pop with a baby in my belly, and to say sex was at the bottom of my list of priorities is an understatement. I've heard of these mythical women who love sex when they are pregnant. After five pregnancies, I can assure you I am not one of those women. I am more of the *please don't touch me; do you see what happened last time you did* kind of woman.

The podcast, which became one of my favorites, highlighted truths about sex and marriage, including the fact that sex is about more than physical connection. It is great for a couple's connection mentally and spiritually too. After listening to a few episodes, I knew that, even though I was uncomfortably pregnant, it was time to stop hiding behind my belly.

I spent the better part of the day psyching myself up to put the moves on my man after the kids went to bed. Usually by that time, I am exhausted, but I really wanted that connection for both of us, so I was determined to preserve the energy to do it. Literally. It was a weekend, and we have teenagers at home, so it was almost midnight before I was fairly certain everyone was asleep. Aside from the privacy factor, I also needed that time to totally clear my mind of my daily tasks and get into the mental space of sex. Maybe you can relate. People always say that foreplay is important, particularly for women. Some of us just need a little time to clear away the thoughts about what time the dog goes to the vet the next day, when the parent-teacher meeting is, or that bills are due—or whatever. You can imagine that it took me a little bit longer to really start enjoying sex when I was awkwardly seven-and-a-half months pregnant. My huge belly, combined with my racing thoughts, were a lot to contend with. But finally, the house was quiet, my heart determined, and my mind focused on my husband. Just as I stretched one leg over my husband, it crossed my mind to double check the lock on the door. But getting into that position had been difficult enough, so I decided that it was late enough. Everyone was sleeping. The door was fine.

You can guess what happened next.

That door swung wide open. There I was, straddling my husband, seven-and-a-half months pregnant, topless, and unable to move quickly (or at all) to cover up because of the belly. One of my children stood in the doorway, eyes wide like a deer in the headlights. Then those eyes were covered (dramatically, I might add) by hands as if to block those blinding headlights.

"Gross! Don't you lock the door?!" said child complained.

To which Rob promptly replied, "Don't you knock?"

The moment for the connection I craved was gone. I laid in bed crying, certain that we scarred our child for life. Imagine walking in on your parents having sex. On second thought, skip that mental picture. Suffice it to say, it's bad enough to walk in on your parents, but to do so when your mom is ready-to-pop pregnant, well that's a whole new kind of mental scarring. Getting pregnant unexpectedly while raising teens and tweens does shine a bit of light on the fact that Mom and Dad do have sex for fun and not just for procreation. But come on! This is a teaching moment I could have done without.

Why would I share this story that makes me turn red in the face just thinking about it? Because vulnerable moments where we share real, ugly, dirty details of life plug into the hearts of other people. Even if none of your children have ever walked in on you and your husband, you have feared it. And if you have experienced the particular feeling of horror, maybe you feel a little less lousy about not locking the door—because you're not the only one. And if you don't have kids yet, you just imagined how horrified you would have been if you caught your parents in the same situation. No matter how you spin it, my embarrassing story relates to your flawed humanity. It reminds you that even a blonde author who runs a booming business and seems like she has her act together has moments of mortification. And let me tell you, there are way more where that came from, but I'm saving those for the next book.

If you want to connect with people, share something about yourself they may not know just by looking at you. Draw people in—not by sharing your highlights but by sharing your real moments. Let them see the authentic you. I am not suggesting that you have to tell your sex stories to complete strangers like I just did. Reserve that story for the right situation. In the meantime, don't be afraid to let people see and connect with the real you.

Vulnerability and authenticity are traits we love and admire in others. So why is it, then, that we tend to hide behind masks of perfection? We retake selfies until we have the one that perfectly represents the life we want, instead of being present in the life we have. What if instead of taking fifteen selfies until we get it seemingly perfect, we invest that time into creating a reality that we love and desire to be present for? After all, in a social-media-driven world where the majority of pictures posted feature perfect smiles in the best lighting, aren't you most likely to stop on the worn image from 1985 spotlighting the mullet and giant bangs your friend once rocked? You know you love to stop and laugh at the picture of a big mess made by a child or animal while no one was watching.

The real, awkward, embarrassing, imperfect moments of life are what draw us together and make us think, *I can relate to that! I really like her. She's just as goofy, messy, or messed up as me!* When you show up as you—imperfect, flawed, unsophisticated you—online or in person, you can capture people's hearts and maybe even make a new friend. So what does being authentic and vulnerable look like?

If you are waiting to start looking for a relationship until you are your ideal weight, stop waiting. Anyone who is in good, physical shape will tell you they can still see their physical flaws if that's where they choose to focus. Find the person who loves you now, in this package.

If you are waiting to have a girls' night in your home until the honey-do list is done or until last season's decorations are put up, stop waiting. Do life with people now—just as you are. Just as *they* are. Inviting people into your home means showing them what home looks like to you—lived in, dusty, maybe a room or two in shambles. They aren't coming for the decorations; they are coming for the connection.

If you are the kind of person who won't leave the house without make-up on, I dare you to put down the makeup brushes and go out in public with a naked face and smile at the people around you. Watch as folks respond with a smile, even when you aren't dressed to impress. It's about connection, not perfection.

When you take off the mask of perfection and interact with people as the "real you," you'll discover that there was no need for the mask in the first place. People prefer you just as God created you. That's a self-esteem booster right there! But opening yourself to authentic relationships is a gift to not just you but also to the people with whom you are engaging. They take pride in knowing the real you. And your refreshing example of authenticity will inspire them to take off their own masks.

If you are going to live your best life, you must be courageous enough to be your truest self. That means being unashamed of who you are and giving others the freedom to be equally authentic with their lives. With authenticity comes trust, and with trust comes an environment free of judgment and full of love. It is in those kinds of relationships that we can forgive—ourselves and others—and feel the grace that comes from knowing we don't have to measure up to anyone else to be "enough."

Some of the most beautiful stories in the Bible are those where Jesus saw people in their most vulnerable state and loved them in spite of their flaws. Jesus showed up each day, sure and completely unashamed of who He was, even though He wasn't what people expected of a king or savior. And through His authentic love and grace, He enabled the people he engaged with to see that they had worth and value.

One of my favorite examples of this love and grace in action is in the story of the woman at the well in John 4. Jesus stopped at a well to rest after a long day of traveling. A Samaritan woman happened to be at the well at the same time, and He asked her for a drink of water. She was surprised that Jesus, a Jewish man, would speak to her at all, much less ask her for a drink of water. As they talked, Jesus told her to go get her husband. The woman replied, "I have no husband."

"That's right," Jesus said. "You have had five husbands, and the man you are with now is not your husband." In those few words, Jesus revealed that He knew her. He knew about her long list of failed relationships and her deep need to be loved. She tried to change the conversation and turn the spotlight off her failures. But Jesus—who spoke to her when the cultural expectation would have been for Him to completely ignore her—revealed the truth about Himself to her. In fact, it was in this conversation that Jesus first told *anyone* (that we know of), that He was the Savior the world had been waiting for. Later in the chapter, we read that because Jesus saw and loved her (flaws and all), she told her whole town about Him. After everyone came out to meet Jesus and hear what He had to say, John tells us, "They said to the woman, 'We no longer believe just because of what you said; now we have heard for ourselves, and we know that this man really is the Savior of the world.'"

Jesus knew that woman and loved her anyway. He knows *you* better than you know yourself—and despite every imperfection, He loves you so much that He made a way for you to be adopted into God's family (Ephesians 1:5). If the One who knows us to the core of our soul loves us just as we are, broken and scarred, we have nothing to fear. And we can let His light shine through the cracks in our masks. Better yet, we can remove our masks and let His light of freedom, forgiveness, and grace shine on others.

Chapter 7
Shiny Spots

*M*y parents divorced when I was a baby, so I have no recollection of them together. My earliest memories of my dad are snapshots from spending weekends at his house and, later, of spending my summers with him and my stepmom in California. I know there's a fairytale stereotype of the evil stepmother, but that was never my experience. I love my stepmom—always have. She is one of the greatest women I know. But no matter how much I loved her, I always dreamed of having a "whole family"—not one that was "broken." I wanted the kind of family I saw in the movies or like my cousins had in their home. I wanted my parents to live together and love each other—and not to fight.

When I was six, my stepmom gave birth to my baby brother, Scott. I adored him immediately. He was so cute, and his tiny toes fascinated me! I was thrilled to be a big sister. I loved the idea of a little person looking up to me. But then, just as quickly as Scott was born, my dad and his new family moved to California. To a six-year-old, California might as well have been Mars. I went from seeing my dad every few days to seeing him at Christmas and for one month each summer. From my tiny view, everyone seemed to be just fine with my dad being far away. I, however, was devastated. I longed for time with my dad. I missed the days when he lived nearby, and we could pick strawberries from the garden together. I missed watching him chase down a chicken for dinner so he could show us the real meaning of "running around like a chicken with its head cut off."

I missed the warm days swinging on the front porch while he played his guitar and sang to me. Now I spent recess on the swings, pumping my legs to get as high as I could—hoping that if I went high enough, I could see to California. I made up a song just for him that, to this day, still occasionally swirls around in my head. I thought maybe one day I could teach it to him so he could play it on his guitar. It went like this: "Daddy, come back to me, where you used to be, so I can see you even more. Daddy come back to me, where you used to be, so I can love you even more."

I wondered why my dad didn't love me enough to stay. *Why did he love my little brother and stepmom more?* I wondered what I did or didn't do that made him want to leave me. *Was I unlovable? Was I too much responsibility?* Adolescence turned my heartbreak and confusion into anger and bitterness. *Why didn't my parents try harder to keep their marriage together? Why didn't they think about us?* And for good measure, I threw in a bit of jealousy. *Why was my older brother doing just fine?* He seemed to be thriving with good grades and athleticism. Since I couldn't compete with my brother academically or in sports, I decided to make my own mark on the world. It just wasn't in the right places.

I found a crowd of friends, which looked a lot like the gang from the Island of Misfit Toys on the Claymation *Rudolph the*

Red-Nosed Reindeer. I seemed to be skilled in finding friends who had encountered all the hard knocks in life. Their choices often reflected the lack of guidance in their homes—and I was easily influenced. Like a sponge, I absorbed everything I heard.

Throughout my childhood, people I trusted—my grandparents, aunts, and cousins—tried to comfort me by sharing their opinions about my dad. They told me stories of a man whose actions were selfish, cowardly, and unloving. They allowed me to believe that I was better off without him in my life. As I looked at him through their eyes, what I didn't see was the anger they harbored toward him because of the hurt they felt from the divorce. I used those stories and my own sense of desperate loss to encircle my father in a trap from which he couldn't escape. Every action (or inaction) he chose magnified his monstrosity in my mind. As I got older and shared my story with my teenage friends, their support further fueled my anger and hurt. I burned with rage, and there's no doubt that my dad saw the flames and felt the fire. I did anything I could to hurt him the way he had hurt me, including spitting bitter words at him anytime he was around.

Anger and rebellion became my identity. My friends began to count on me to be the one to fight for what I believed in (even if it was wrong). My gift for words became my weapon, and often the words were brash and led me to detention, where I am pretty sure they had a permanent desk for me. I turned to alcohol and promiscuity to numb my pain. Not surprisingly, I struggled with most of my relationships, bouncing back and forth between obsession and flippancy. I longed to be loved but was too afraid to love back, believing that I would do something to cause the other person to leave me—just like I did my dad. When I finally did love and it wasn't returned, I became obsessive trying to control people's emotions, forcing them to love me on my terms.

My parents' divorce shaped me. With an average of 2,400 divorces occurring per day in the United States,[1] I know that I'm not alone in the sense of loss and desperation I felt as a child and teenager. And I know that some kids handle things better, or at least differently, than I did. I'm also well aware that I can be a bit dramatic. But just like each different type of metal has its own melting point, we all respond differently to the heat life puts on us. Lead melts at 621°F, while platinum holds out to 3220°F. For a long time, I didn't understand how my brother could take the heat without missing a step while I, on the other hand, swung unpredictably from melting to exploding. As I matured, I began to understand how God uses the struggles we experience to show us who He is. And we can see Him most clearly when we are at our weakest. He uses each fire we walk through as an opportunity to shape us. If we allow Him to lead the way to healing, those painful experiences can mold us into the people He created us to be. I can see how God used my hurt and even my poor choices to help me come to know Him, but it took years for me to become aware of what He was doing in my life.

By the time I was a young adult, I had built a protective wall around my heart so high there was no way my dad could get through it. I lived more than twenty-five years of my life angry at him, never once asking him for his account of the stories I had been told. I never considered asking him why he left; I just assumed I understood. I was comfortable behind the wall I had built and saw no reason to come out.

Eventually, my dad moved back to Illinois so he could be present for the final years of his parents' lives. His move took away the convenient excuse of distance, and I felt forced into allowing him to build a relationship with my children. I hesitated when he asked to visit because I feared he would leave again one day and hurt them the way he hurt me. But even though we barely knew each other, I could see the joy my children brought him each time we got together. I often wondered if his apology to me was written through the love he showed my kids. My response to him and his presence in our lives continued to swing between anger and love; I wanted to forgive him, but I didn't know how. Aside from that, I was too caught up in raising my young family to invest any significant emotional energy into our damaged relationship. Even so, those embers of hurt continued to smolder, affecting every relationship I encountered.

My unaddressed fears about my dad caused repetitive nightmares. I would dream that Rob was cheating on me or that he was leaving me. The worst part was that, in those nightmares, Rob would flippantly tell me, "I'm out," and wish me luck—as if leaving me didn't bother him at all. They were only dreams, and when I was awake, I could rationalize that they were a depiction of what I thought it had been like for my dad to leave us. I had convinced myself my father had left us with no internal battle and no regrets. Unfortunately, those nightmares and my fear of them coming true wound into our day-to-day lives. The anger I had felt toward my father as a teen raged against my marriage. Every little argument felt as if it would end in divorce. I began to question whether Rob had ever really loved me, and I worked hard to make sure I was perfect all the time so that he wouldn't leave me. The more I strove for perfection, the greater my fears grew because I noticed every imperfection. I had enough self-awareness to see that my unresolved "daddy issues" were going to cost me everything if I didn't sort them out, but again, I wasn't sure what to do. *Who was I if I wasn't an angry girl, victimized by the crappy hand life had dealt me?*

That's when I felt a nudging in my heart. I had heard you should pray for your enemies, and I thought it was worth a try. *Besides*, I thought, *my dad needs all the prayer he can get.* Matthew 5:44 (KJV) states, "*But I say unto you, Love your enemies, bless them that curse you, do good to them that hate you, and pray for them which despitefully use you, and persecute you.*" So I began praying for the enemy I had constructed in my heart over the years. I prayed for my dad to have a changed heart toward me because I believed he was embarrassed and ashamed of me. I wasn't sure if he liked me, let alone if he loved me. I thought that if his actions changed, surely I would be cured from my heartache and those nightmares. Mostly I prayed he would apologize. I had convinced myself I had done nothing wrong, forgetting that in my hurt, I had done and said things that certainly required apology and healing.

> "But I say unto you, Love your enemies, bless them that curse you, do good to them that hate you, and pray for them which despitefully use you, and persecute you."
> —Matthew 5:44 (KJV)

In sixth grade, my mom caught me kissing a fifteen-year-old boy behind the library in our little town. Just after that, I was caught smoking a cigarette stolen from one of my misfit friends' parents. And when I didn't make the cheerleading squad that year (which I saw as my only hope for ever being "popular"), I threatened to take a bottle of ibuprofen. My threat, like so much of my behavior, was a plea for attention. (Clearly, raising me was no walk in the park.) Shortly after the suicide threat, my parents made a joint decision that I would go live with my dad in St. Louis for a while. They sprung the news on me while I was at his house for what I thought was a quick visit. With all the fiery anger that had built up in my adolescent heart, I fought the only way I knew how: with my words. I cussed my dad up one side and down the other. I told him exactly how much I hated him and all he represented in my life. If hatred was my fuel, I could have flown to the moon. Like many adults who saw my fire, my dad tried to fight my fire with fire instead of with love. He didn't know what else to do.

As a parent of five children, I know how hard it can be to act lovingly toward children who push you away. I was a child when I unleashed my anger on my dad, but I knew what I was doing. I wanted to hurt him. When I started to pray for my dad, I started to remember all the things I needed to apologize to him for, but I wasn't ready to admit my faults just yet.

In John 13, Jesus takes time to wash the feet of his disciples. I am not a Bible scholar, so I don't know the exact history of what people's feet looked like in Bible times. I have, however, been to Haiti a few times and have seen the feet of people who walk barefoot all day—everywhere. Dirt and grime under unkept, thick toenails, calluses encompassing the ball of the foot, and cracks where the moisture slipped out at the heel. I am not talking about how your feet look when you have gone too long between pedicures. I am talking about some cracked, coarse, and dirty feet.

Now imagine the Son of the Great King washing those feet.

If you have a hard time picturing Jesus stooping to wash your feet, then think about the dreamiest celebrity you can. Come on, we all have a fan crush. Mine happens to be Joey McIntyre from my favorite boy band, New Kids on the Block. And I know that if Joey Mac walked into a room and said, "Hey, girl! I want to wash your feet," my response would be, "Uhhhhh . . . never going to happen. Not in a million years." I don't care how recent the pedicure. But if he asked me to wash his, I would at least consider it. Feet on anyone older than two years old gross me out, but I've been waiting for Joey to confess his love to me since I was eight years old, so there's a strong possibility that I'd grab a towel and tell him to have a seat.

These men knew that Jesus was the Messiah—the Son of God—and despite His position of power, He wanted to wash *their* feet. Later in the evening, He told them that one of them would betray Him yet. He already knew who was going to betray Him, but He cleaned *everyone's* feet, not just those of the apostles whom He knew would be loyal. In John 13:14–17 (NIV), Jesus finished washing their feet and said, "Now that I, your Lord and Teacher, have washed your feet, you also should wash one another's feet. I have set you an example that you should do as I have done for you. Very truly I tell you, no servant is greater than his master, nor is a messenger greater than the one who sent him. Now that you know these things, you will be blessed if you do them."

The more I prayed for my dad, the more convicted I felt about my part in our broken relationship. As the Holy Spirit worked on my heart, my prayers shifted. Instead of praying that my dad's heart and actions would change, I began to pray that *my* heart would change. I asked God to reveal my responsibility for this battle in my heart. I knew that, as a child, I acted out of immature emotions and behaved in ways that may have even seemed justified to my friends and family members. But now I was an adult, and it was time for me to take ownership for my part in the wreckage. It was time for me to accept the fact that I couldn't change the way other people behaved, but I could change my own responses and behaviors. I was tired of being angry and exhausted from trying to control the rage and manipulate my emotions. I wanted a change that would last and was ready to do whatever it took.

In my marriage, almost every fight between Rob and me could be traced back to my inability to trust or to my fear of abandonment. When I began to pray for God to change my heart regarding my relationship with my dad, the Holy Spirit moved fast and fierce in this area of my life too. Less than a week later, a Sunday morning church service turned into a miracle delivered just for me. This isn't the kind of miracle we read about in the Bible. No one regained their sight or went from lame to leaping in the literal sense, but the moment felt miraculous, nonetheless. I don't even remember what the sermon was about; I just remember it piercing my heart like nothing I had ever known. Every ounce of anger and bitterness drained out of me through tears. It was an ugly cry, people, the kind that leaves you gasping for air and makes those around you wonder if they should hug you or pretend like everything is fine. When we got in the car, Rob looked at me and said, "So are you going to go talk to your dad or what?"

I drove to his house that afternoon, unsure of what I would say or how I would say it when I got there. It didn't really matter; I could already feel the relief from the fire of anger that had burned inside me for so long. When we started talking, I asked my dad questions, and he and my stepmom shared the heartache of leaving my brother and me behind to find a way to provide for us. My dad shared his regret in his decisions and his own painful childhood scars that prompted his own tough choices. It was the first day in years where I had seen my father as a human: frail, weak, and needing Jesus's forgiveness just like me. I set aside my expectations, began deconstructing the wall around my heart. I listened to his side of the story and understood that he was, like me, a product of a fallen world. He was a man who had loved and failed and learned and ached because of difficult decisions and choices. He wasn't the evil villain I had characterized him to be; he was just a man, doing his best in the moment.

That conversation marked the beginning of healing. That healing paved the way for me to have whole, healthy relationships. It was on this day that the FOG began to lift from my heart. By taking that one step toward forgiveness, I began to see more clearly how fears had crept into my life and tainted everything.

Leaning into and living in forgiveness rather than fear, however, wasn't a one-time decision; it's a daily action. You can decide to forgive just like you can decide to lose weight, but until you put a meal plan and a workout regimen into action, it's just a decision. To lose weight, you have to do the work of exercising and eating right—and it takes time to see the results. The same is true when it comes to forgiveness.

> Leaning into and living in forgiveness rather than fear, however, wasn't a one-time decision; it's a daily action.

The day I took the step toward forgiving my dad, I thought I could lay it all down, turn the page, and start a new chapter. I took the action to forgive my dad that Sunday afternoon, but it took much longer for my daily actions and emotional responses—behaviors and habits that had been set into motion years earlier—to catch up with my newfound resolve.

Here's the thing: When you have been ticked off for *years*, anger becomes a habit. For years, I had doubted whether I could trust myself to love and to be loved. For years, fear-fueled anger was my first response to any conflict or confrontation. Breaking those habits took time and intention. Seeing myself as someone more than an angry girl with a quick temper and sharp tongue took *a lot* of time.

People who know me well joke that I see people's "shiny spots." These are the spots that reveal what's under the dirt and grime we all carry. No matter how flawed someone is, I see a person's potential. This trait can be a blessing and curse. It's how my mom ended up with a houseful of flea-infested stray cats and a slew of garage sale toys to give to friends. If I found someone who seemed worse off than me and I could love them, it left me hoping that even girls like me had shiny spots. Even as a child, I found it easy to see other people's shiny spots. But as I embarked on my journey of healing, I wondered if there were any shiny spots hiding under the armor I'd worn for so long.

I kept praying for God to change my heart, and He faithfully delivered friends, who acted as guides and sounding boards as I walked through the healing process. As frightening as it felt to be vulnerable, I knew I needed to forgive myself as much as I needed to forgive my dad. This, too, had to be more than a decision. I had to take action. Here are some steps I needed to take to get through forgiveness of both my father and myself.

- I asked a few trusted friends and family members to give me two or three words or phrases they would use to describe me. It was enlightening to see myself through the eyes of others. Where I saw rebellion, they saw courage. Where I saw "talks too much," they saw articulate.
- I needed to grasp that I was not my father or mother, but I was wholly me. So I listed character traits that I liked in both of my parents and then listed things I liked in me. I took note of things that matched up and things that were unique to me. It was refreshing to remind myself that I didn't have to be exactly like anyone except me.
- I immersed myself in personal development. Books, seminars, and personality tests, such as StrengthsFinder 2.0 and Enneagram, became pivotal. These growth-minded quizzes reminded me to look at who I am now because of where I came from, which allowed me to embrace the past and love who I am now.

I also knew that if I simply moved toward forgiveness, step-by-step, that God would handle the rest. But I was still afraid, and fear makes us do funny things—even when we're old enough to know better.

If you are ever in the doctor's office when my oldest son is there for a vaccine booster, please don't be alarmed. It may sound as if the apocalypse is near, and he is fighting for his life. When the shouting doesn't work, he shrinks into a corner in an attempt to hide. This teenager regresses at least eight years and starts calling me "Mommy" like a five-year-old. He holds his arms tightly to his body, and tears well up in his eyes; it's full panic mode. I, being the loving mother that I am, tell him to man up and get his scaredy-cat, little butt up onto the table and take his shot. Then I launch into an obligatory lecture about how it would be much worse to get a deadly disease than to get this silly, little shot. And because he sees the determination in my eyes, he knows he has no choice. He climbs on the table and gets the shot—then laughs at himself and says, "That didn't even hurt, Mom." Wading into my own fear of what I would discover about myself, once I removed my mask of anger and hurt, felt a little like that.

Fear causes us to magnify the uneasiness we feel. We can forget that one, small action forward is much less painful than standing in our own doubt. Once the tiny needle stick is over, it's done. It's freeing. And we giggle and think, *That wasn't so bad.* Each step we take toward forgiveness helps clear a path for healing. It all begins with a prayer asking for God to lift the FOG in our hearts.

We are prideful, angry, bitter, and scared. We are human. God created us knowing we would need to rely on our relationship with Him to experience true peace, love, and patience. If you aren't sure what you believe about God or are perhaps a new Christian, the idea that you have to rely on anyone but yourself may not sit well with you. That feeling is part of our human nature too! We all want to be self-reliant, and that desire can make us think that God is being a little egotistical, wanting us to rely on Him. But let's step back and get a little perspective: God created the earth. The *whole* earth—everything from the tiniest molecule to the design on a butterfly's wings to the raging waterfalls to the specks of color in your son's eyes up to the highest mountain. Everything that has ever prompted you to say "wow" or "amazing"—it's because of God. So perhaps we need to move our own egos aside and realize it's okay for Him to require us to rely on His power and immense love. What He has done is a pretty big deal! And if you think about forgiveness, what He's done *for* the world is an even bigger deal. I know how hard it can be for me to forgive others or myself—how hard it was for me to forgive my dad. My own difficulty with forgiveness makes the reality that Jesus came to earth to forgive every one of us simply amazing. We only have to ask, and He will come and live in our heart and give us a fresh start each minute of the day. He forgives because He Loves us.

2 Corinthians 5:17 (ESV) says, "Therefore, if anyone is in Christ, he is a new creation. The old has passed away; behold, the new has come." Don't just breeze past that scripture and those last few sentences. Let it soak in for a moment. The Creator of this universe loves you enough to forgive you. If you are a follower of Jesus, God looks at you and sees not just your shiny spots but *perfection* because of Jesus.

That love and forgiveness astounds me, considering the number of times I need forgiveness each day. Even more amazing is the truth that I don't have to do anything more than believe in order to receive that forgiveness. There is no amount of good or bad that you or I can do as believers that will change the inheritance God is preparing for us in eternity. Think about it this way: When your kids go the extra mile to do something great, your heart swells with pride, but you do not love them more. You love them because they are your children. And when they drive you crazy or do something that grieves you to the core, you love them because they are your children. God's forgiveness is not a get-out-of-jail-free card or an excuse to sin or a reason to be lazy. It is a gift to those who decide to follow Jesus—a gift that transforms us from the inside out, a gift that has the power to fill us with that peace and love we so desperately crave.

Forgiveness changes everything. It changes the way we see ourselves and the way we see others. God's forgiveness is even greater because it changes how He sees us. The fact that He *wants* us to rely on Him—that He *allows* us to rely on Him—is a gift. If it's hard to understand, that's okay. You and I are human, remember? And God, well, He is the Creator of the universe. I am not so sure I would want His responsibilities. It seems kind of daunting to make the sun rise and set at the perfect time each day. I can hardly decide what time to make dinner most days. Lean into the forgiveness He offers and accept the gift—even if you feel like you don't deserve it. Because the truth is, none of us do.

Chapter 8
Finding the Right Relationships

*I*n the previous chapter, we talked about the gift of forgiveness. Relationships are the reason behind that amazing gift. God created you for relationship. First and foremost, He wants a relationship with you. He designed you with a need for relationships—and that, too, is a gift. In fact, I believe relationships are one of the most rewarding gifts God gives us. They are also one of the most challenging aspects of life.

Think about the nights you've spent with friends laughing until you cry. No matter how much you try to recreate that night with the same people, same scenario, you'll never be able to duplicate that experience. Moments like that are a gift from your Maker. They are crafted just for you to fill your heart with joy. We crave that kind of joy-filled connection because we were created for it! Those simple, precious moments are a picture of the kind of joy

Jesus finds in relationship with each of us. Whether you are an introvert, extrovert, or somewhere in between, the gift of relationship brings richness and joy to your life!

You may be thinking, *What about the bad relationships—the kind that cause heartache?* If rich, loving relationships are a gift, are dysfunctional relationships created as a form of punishment? The answer to that question is a big N-O! God isn't interested in punishing you, but He is interested in refining you, like a diamond. Diamonds are created from an unlikely substance when just the right amount of time, pressure, and heat are applied to it. The learning you gain from difficult relationships—or from difficult times in good relationships—may not be fun. It may even be a painful process, but those relationships can help you become the beautiful jewel you were meant to be.

John 15:13 (NIV) says, "Greater love has no one than this: to lay down one's life for one's friends." This verse is a beautiful picture of a friend who is loyal and loving. True, deep, and lasting relationships require our selflessness at times—laying aside our wants to meet someone else's needs. Marriage is one relationship that gives us plenty of opportunities to practice this. My husband and I have known each other since fifth grade. We started "going steady" in junior high, and within three short months, our relationship had become a record for me—and I was the only girlfriend he ever had. We have experienced times of sheer joy and moments of agony. We even had dramatic blow ups, like the time when Rob looked right at me and shouted, "I quit you!"—to which I said something like, "No! I quit you first!" We were thirteen, and drama was a way of life. Today, of course, we can laugh at that part of our story, and we often marvel at how God guided us through the years. We recently told our daughter that we met in fifth grade, and she was shocked and horrified at the thought that she might already know the person she will marry. I assured her that it was rare, then I took a minute to thank God for the gift, the hardships, heartaches, and incredible joys my husband and I have experienced together over these years.

You've heard the saying, "'Tis better to have loved and lost than to have never loved at all." The person who first said this obviously walked through the murky waters of pained relationships and woke up wiser—and more sparkly, like a diamond. But no one enjoys that feeling of loss. We spend countless hours on social media trying to fill our need for relationship. We've been tricked into believing the romanticized ideas we have seen in books and movies. While lifelong friendships are beautiful, it is rare for two people to remain connected in morals and values. People grow, change, have new experiences, get new jobs, and have children at different times. Good friends morph into acquaintances with no one to blame—and there are some relationships you may need to be intentional about leaving behind. You have likely wandered in and out of countless relationships in your lifetime. But most of your friendships will have a full, beautiful season, then just like summer fades into fall, they'll fade. You may have only one or two forever friends in your life, so when you find them, cherish those rare gems as the gifts they are!

Through the years, there have been seasons when I have had to examine the relationships closest to me. Proverbs 4:23 (NIV) warns us, "Above all else, guard your heart, for everything you do flows from it." Who and what you allow into your heart influences who you become. That truth applies to the movies you watch and the books you read—as well as to the people with whom you surround yourself. What goes in must come out. We know this is true for our children; it's why we carefully censor our children's intake of movies and music. What goes into their brains comes out through their mouths! I remember when my oldest daughter was just old enough to start figuring out the difference between boys and girls. During bath time, I took a moment to point out how her and her brother were anatomically different. It seemed like a simple enough lesson, until we were at the park the next day, and I overheard her asking each of the neighborhood kids if they had a penis or a vagina. Information had gone into her brain and was flowing right out of her young mouth.

As adults, our ability to filter what comes of our mouths improves (Wouldn't parties be awkward if it didn't!), but the reality is that when we read books, watch movies, or spend time with friends who are vulgar or negative, we tend to mimic what we see and hear. Motivational speaker Jim Rohn said we are the average of the five people we spend the most time with. Think for a moment: Excluding your children (because legally you have to spend time with them), who are your five people? Every now and then, it's healthy to reevaluate your relationships. Take a deep dive into each of your five closest relationships and ask yourself if you are willing to be the sum of what each person represents. You don't just get to choose their good qualities and leave the bad ones behind. Just like two plus two doesn't get to be half of four, you don't get to be parts of the whole. I am not talking about judging your friends but rather giving your relationship a grade. If the relationship isn't helping you grow, or perhaps it's making you wither, it may be time to reconsider why you are still nurturing it. What relationships do you feel obligated to maintain? Maybe it's a family member, a mom, sister, or childhood friend that you feel like you are stuck with for life. Maybe you can identify this friend as a coworker that you tolerate on girls' night because you feel like you have no other choice. Or maybe you have a friend who had a lot of hard knocks in life, and you feel they deserve some grace even if it is at the expense of your mental and emotional well-being. Here's a hint: If you feel stuck or trapped, the relationship isn't healthy. History or family connections can make us feel as if we have no way out of a relationship. It's easy to get stuck in the romanticized belief that a particular friendship was made to last a lifetime—when maybe its season has come and gone. It's okay to let go and move forward. I'm not promising that letting go will be easy, but I do promise it's okay to do so.

> **Here's a hint: If you feel stuck or trapped, the relationship isn't healthy.**

My rule for myself is to spend time with people who I aspire to be more like. That doesn't mean my friends are perfect, but it means that I use my moral compass to choose my friends. Proverbs 18:24 (NIV) is true that "one who has unreliable friends soon comes to ruin, but there is a friend who sticks closer than a brother." We have a perfect friend in Jesus, but no other relationship will be flawless. And yes, we need to extend grace to those who have hurt us, ourselves included. No relationship is free of human faults. But we also need to guard our hearts and be aware of what a healthy amount of imperfection in a relationship looks like. The forgiveness we talked about in the previous chapter is important for every relationship in our lives. Forgiveness sets our hearts free so that we can develop healthy, rich friendships. But forgiveness doesn't mean anything goes. Even as we forgive, we must set boundaries on what we allow into our hearts and lives. Otherwise, we'll end up allowing so-called friends to turn us into people we don't like.

One thing that surprises me the most about my work is how often I help adult women learn to recognize and maneuver unhealthy relationships. Women (in fact, all humans) desperately want to be loved. Following that desire, we throw ourselves into unhealthy relationships, acting as if it's a game to see whether we can win over the most challenging people. I get it: Finding friends as an adult is hard! But if we aren't intentional about what we allow in our lives, unhealthy relationships can tear us down from the inside out.

We tend to tolerate unhealthy relationships, unknowingly letting them steal our energy. We have the friend who is flaky; she says she will show up but then cancels last minute. Or the relationship that always leaves you irritated and muttering, "I cannot believe she just said that to me." Many women put up with one-sided relationships that take advantage of our giving spirit. Or on the flip side, we allow people into our lives who are constantly keeping score, expecting us to do for them what they did for us in exact balance and proportion.

Healthy relationships are built on loyalty, trust, and giving without expectation. Most great relationships are not problem-free, but they are strong and can withstand hard conversations. Recognize the relationships that come with healthy challenge. Proverbs 27:17 (NIV) says, "As iron sharpens iron, so one person sharpens another." I imagine this verse and think if I were the piece of iron involved in the sharpening, it wouldn't always feel great, but it would always leave me sharper, shinier, and stronger than I started. Don't mistake a good friend as someone who is always nice to you. Many people can be nice but may not have the best intentions for your growth. Sometimes kindness shows up in tough love or real truths. Kindness shows up when a friend or family member encourages you to step outside of your comfort zone to follow a dream. Or kindness shows up in the friend who appears on your doorstep and takes the kids for the night so that you and your husband can have a date (even when you don't think you need one). A nice friend wants to make you feel good, but a kind friend does what makes you the best you!

If you aren't intentional in seeking meaningful friendships, you'll never have the opportunity to laugh until you cry. You'll miss out on the spark of joy that happens when you and a friend have an inside joke. You'll miss that incredible sense of belonging and connecting. And most of all, you'll miss the person that you could become because of your healthy, meaningful friendship.

I don't know about you, but I miss my junior high years. Sure. Braces and acne make life awkward, but making friends was easy! A large percentage of the people around you were just like you. They grew up in a similar neighborhood, had siblings close to the same ages, liked mostly the same afterschool activities, and spent their evenings doing the exact same homework as you. You had ways to connect. You had common ground.

When we leave school, we suddenly realize how ill-prepared we are to find friends in the real world. You go from spending the majority of your time with people just like you to a work situation with a man who oddly reminds you of your dentist (mostly because you remember that your dentist also had large nose hairs) and a woman who strangely resembles a character from a 1990s *Saturday Night Live* skit. (Please tell me I'm not alone here!) There's no common ground with those people, aside from the fact that you have the same employer, attend the same church, or go to the same coffee shop. I can't count the number of times as an adult, in small groups for church, work situations, or other social gatherings, where I have looked around and thought, *How on earth did I get here? How am I supposed to connect with this person on a deeper level? We have nothing in common.*

The first time I experienced this feeling was right after college. I had had big plans to move back to my hometown in Illinois, where many of my closest friends and family members still lived. I imagined hanging out with my girlfriends and "officially" starting a life with Rob. Rob turned those plans upside down when he called to tell me he was moving to Wisconsin! We had never talked about living anywhere other than Illinois, and if we were going to move somewhere, surely it would be south where we could enjoy the sunshine. He lured me into his plans by sending me a magazine article boasting Sheboygan County as "The Best Place in the United States to Raise a Family." While I wasn't ready to raise a family yet, I thought being in a town with such a status would get him into proposal mode! I agreed and quickly found an internship. Two days after I graduated from college, I moved up to Wisconsin and started life as an adult. What a rude awakening! Turns out the best place in the United States to raise a family is actually full of families . . . you know, with young children. It was nothing like the college town we had just left. The people I worked with were nice, but conversations quickly died when we got past the weather. Rob adjusted well to our new town because his internship put him in a place where he was surrounded by other new college graduates. But I had never felt more alone. I was young, single, and didn't quite mesh with the people around me who were all raising families and running to afterschool activities. I had a bachelor's degree in communications and had no idea how to communicate with people who were different than me.

I would love to finish this story with some beautiful, teachable plan of how I met friends, but I don't have one. While I knew people and we would meet couples out for dinner and drinks, I never really found the kind of friend I was hoping for. I did nothing intentional to meet friends while we were in Wisconsin. I spent a lot of time whining about the results I didn't get from work I wasn't willing to do. You can't just hope you get the six-pack abs, the medal for finishing the race, or good friends to spend your time with. You have to be purposeful in the pursuit of your heart's desires.

The adjustment from college to real life left me feeling lost and confused. I bounced from job to job because I was discontent and unchallenged. It was years later when I found myself lonely and looking for good friends. Determined to build my own tribe of friends, I began putting some of my business practices in place.

To be successful in business, you have to be deliberate with your goals. Why would finding friends be any different?

When you go out fishing, you don't expect fish to just jump into your boat. You have to cast a line, and the more lines you cast, the more likely you'll catch a fish. As with all good fishing excursions, you may get some small fish that need thrown back, but the hope is that the more lines you cast, the more likely you'll get a few keepers. The interesting thing about finding friends is that women, as a whole, are lonely and looking for friendships. Once you start willfully looking for friendships, you'll find that many women are in the same boat as you—lonely and hoping for real connection. Here are some simple tips on how I built my own tribe of women who support me and lift me up in life.

- Put down your phone, book, planner, or whatever else you stare at when you are at kids' events or the park. I mean, put it totally and completely away! Instead of engaging in the virtual world, drifting off into another world or planning next week, stay in this moment and look to see if anyone around you might be someone to engage with. Sure, you're using your time wisely, but we are looking for something to fill your energy, not your time. Good conversation charges your soul.

- Choose your seat wisely and change them often at all events you attend regularly. Church, ball games, conferences, or meetings; find a seat next to someone you have never sat next to before. Simply being next to someone and asking things like, "Which child is yours?" or saying, "That sermon was amazing" can spark conversation, and conversation can lead to friendships.

- Learn that it's not weird to ask someone if you can find them on social media. This is where technology is our friend!

Connect with someone at a banquet or the gym yesterday? Awesome! Tell them you enjoyed their company, ask them when they regularly attend, and then ask if you can find them on social media. I might say something like, "What did you say your name was? I've enjoyed working out with you today; you seem like a lot of fun! Do you always come to this class? Could we connect on social media so we can plan to meet here again? I'm new in town, and I am trying to make some connections to other women."

- Join the club, meeting, Bible study, or new gym in town. Whatever it is, don't be afraid to join something new. When we first moved back to Illinois, I joined a mom's group, and it saved my life! It's so cool because thirteen years later, I am still connected to many of the women I met in that group.

- Stop waiting for someone to invite you to something and instead create your own event. Plan a girls' night out. Reach out to a few women who you'd like to get to know better and ask them to join you for margaritas, chips, and salsa on Thursday night. Don't make this a strings-attached kind of invitation, so things like a Thirty-One party or a something similar (where you are asking her to buy something so you can get something free) doesn't count. And remember, that's my job, and I still say it doesn't count! That's not the right way to make friends, but it is the right way to connect with old friends. When you are trying to build your tribe, a simple getting-to-know-you, let's-have-some-laughs kind of night is all you need!

In my attempt to meet some friends in my adult life, I learned some valuable lessons in finding the right friends. Insecurity and awkwardness replaced the spontaneous, fun girl of my college years. It wasn't until Rob and I moved back to Illinois that I finally found my first friend as an adult. We met at a holiday party Rob and I had been invited to, and Carli and I hit it off immediately. She was charismatic and witty and reminded me of a carefree time in my life before my world was ruled by spit-up and diaper changes. Carli came along at a time when I really needed a friend. Rob and I had recently moved back "home" from Wisconsin, and I had dreamed of moving back to Illinois for so long that I'd built up a fantasy of coming home to a bunch of friends who had been missing me. They would welcome me with open arms to girls' night out and Sunday movies. Instead, I found old friends who were living in a different season of life than me. I was the first of my childhood friends to get married and have children.

While I still longed for the twenty-something nightlife, my reality included waking up three times a night to feed my two babies. Carli gave me something to look forward to during long weeks as a stay-at-home mom. She understood that a night out could sometimes consist of going to the local fast food playland! It was a relief for me to finally have someone who understood my crazy world, wanted to be part of it, and was still up for girl time and an occasional glass of wine. Carli was the best kind of friend. She would bring me meals when I was having a bad day, pray with me, and we would watch each other's kids so we could each get a break. She helped me find my fun-loving side again by encouraging me to do things like go to concerts and have girls' nights to escape the burdens of motherhood for short time periods. Carli and I were inseparable. I felt like Carli rescued me. I dreamed of this friendship being one that would be years in the making, where our children would get married and we would be in-laws. I had plans for this friendship to last a lifetime!

If a woman meets a man in a grocery store and he punches her or knocks her down right there in the store, is she going to go on a date with him? Of course not! He doesn't start out being violent and abusive. He woos her first, bringing her into his web. He shows her all of the greatness he has to offer, and after she has seen how good he can be and how much she needs him in her life, she falls in love. It's after she sees how great he can be that the controlling and abusive behavior begins. She is taken aback and hopeful that the abuse is just a phase. The relationship that started like a dream ends up being a nightmare.

Beauty and charm can be deceiving. Satan doesn't look like a monster or even like a man with horns wearing a red suit. Satan is actually described in the Bible in Ezekiel 28:14–18 as beautiful, wise, even blameless until he became corrupt and violent. His beauty lures people in and blinds them to reality. He leaves his prey wondering what's wrong with them or where they went astray. That's what happened with Carli and me.

I noticed a few red flags with Carli early on, but I didn't think much of them at first. The biggest thing I noticed was that Carli aired people's dirty laundry frequently. She didn't just talk about people who got on her nerves or make snide comments about strangers. She was downright nasty about people whom she considered friends. Her words were like one of those roasts you see comedians doing: true and funny, but done without permission and revealing real wounds and imperfections in others' lives. I *knew* that, since I was on Carli's good side, I would never be the butt of her jokes. Often after we hung out together, I felt guilty and ashamed. I was afraid that her other friends (whom I really liked) would find out that I had laughed at Carli's jokes at their expense. And there were times when I would participate or agree with Carli. I lowered myself to Carli's standards and joined in, even though I knew it was wrong. I was afraid to lose the friendship, and after going without a friend for so long, that fear was worse than the guilt and shame I felt.

Carli soon started taking jabs at me. Saying things like, "I know I'm your best friend, but you're not really mine, and that's okay," or "I'm clearly a better Christian than you, but . . ." I didn't just let her comments roll off my back; I took her words to heart, trying harder to be a better friend and Christian. At the time, I was a new Christian and was still learning about what that even meant. Carli baffled me; she knew Scripture well, but her drinking (which went from the occasional glass of wine to several glasses too many) and cruel jokes seemed to counteract what she professed to believe. We did everything together—book clubs, we shared friends, our kids loved playing together, she started working with me, and even our husbands were friends. Standing up for myself or others when she made a cruel comment seemed to make life difficult, so I made excuses for Carli, justifying her actions based on what I knew about her history. I took the blame, thinking I was somehow at fault for the way she started talking to me. Maybe I was too much. Maybe I should back off a little. I enjoyed spending time with her. Maybe that was weird. I had noticed the way Carli's other friends started looking at me, and I knew Carli had started her own whispering campaign about me.

After several uncomfortable instances with her friends' awkward gazes, I realized I was never an exception to the rule; I had never been safe from Carli's harsh words. She spoke about me to her other friends, the same way she spoke about them to me. My visits with Carli left me feeling naked, exposed, vulnerable, and fearful about what judgments she was forming. Our plans together caused anxiety and irritability. I ended up crying before and after our visits. When the phone rang and Carli's name popped up on the screen, my stomach would sink, but I would still answer. Many of the conversations would leave me distracted from my children and focused on this failing relationship. Pictures of Carli and her new best friends on social media cut deep. When Carli held parties,

I drank more than normal because that's what everyone else was doing, and I desperately wanted to fit in and have our friendship go back to how it used to be. My values went out the window with my self-esteem. I resorted back to the days when swearing and smoking fueled me instead of Jesus and truth.

Then one day, Rob said, "You do realize that every time Carli upsets you, we all pay for it, right?" Leave it to the man of few words to hit me with the words that moved me most. It was the first time I realized that this "friendship" was poisoning every aspect of my life. When I felt anxious about our conversations, I was annoyed and short-tempered with my kids. When I felt unsure of myself in that friendship, it left me unsure in every relationship I had: my husband, my colleagues, even my parents. When I crossed over my own moral lines, it built a wall between God and me. I realized that, right or wrong, I was laying down my life for someone who wasn't willing to do the same in return.

> Rob said, "You do realize that every time Carli upsets you, we all pay for it, right?" Leave it to the man of few words to hit me with the words that moved me most.

I felt disgusted and frustrated with myself for allowing such a juvenile relationship to control my heart. But I also felt trapped, obligated to our affiliation, and afraid to let go. I stayed in that friendship far longer than I should have because of the obligation I felt to Carli. Once I recognized how hazardous our friendship had become, I began taking note of the patterns when Carli would create unnecessary drama. I noticed that when a big celebration happened for me, she would bring a dark cloud, stealing my sunshine. As with any big decision, I spent time praying about this relationship. I asked God to really open my eyes so I could see clearly with no blinders. As He made it more evident to me that this wasn't my fault, I challenged her. I first tried to respectfully tell her how I felt. When we are faced with any hard discussion about our emotions, it is up to us to share our feelings respectfully; it is up to the person we are confronting to manage the information. After several unreasonable and overly emotional conversations, I decided that it was time to walk completely away from that relationship. I blocked any access she had to me on social media, which would control her knowing when those major life moments were coming. I tried to simply ignore her manipulative text messages and emails that twisted the truth, but seeing those hurtful notes gave me knots in my stomach every time. I cut all ties to her by deleting unread emails and blocking her number on my phone. There were even certain friend groups I had to steer clear of for a while because I knew she would be there. They were hard decisions, difficult moves to make, but being on the other side of that relationship that had such a hold on me, I see everything clearer now. When I see Carli in some social situations, I am always friendly and respectful to her, and in many ways, I am thankful for the friendship we had. It taught me so much about myself. It allowed me to exercise my ability to stand up for myself. And it has given me such a real-life perspective to teach other women how to walk away from toxic relationships.

What relationships do you feel obligated to? Maybe it's your alcoholic mother who belittles you and makes you feel unimportant at holiday gatherings; maybe it's your cubical mate at work who reminds you often of your mistakes; it's possible that your ex-husband is still using your past to manipulate you; or maybe you are like me, and you have a friendship that pushes you outside of your moral compass. Just as I did with Carli, you will stay in your toxic relationships until you realize your worth.

You were actually made by the hand of God; it says so in the Bible (Genesis 1:27). You are also unforgettable (Isaiah 49:15), loved (Jeremiah 31:3), worth fighting for (Romans 5:8), redeemed (1 Peter 1:18, 19), and you have a bright future ahead (Ephesians 2:4–7). Knowing these verses doesn't mean that you will accept them as truth right away. I have many of these verses taped in places like bathroom mirrors, by my scale, and near my computer. I put them in these locations because these are the first places that the truths about me start to fade. I look in the mirror, and the lies and self-doubt begin. Maybe you have other places where you spend time, and self-doubt creeps in; put these verses there! Remind yourself of those truths every day until you believe them.

We haven't been promised a life without challenge, but we have been promised that we are worthy. We haven't been promised that our friends will be perfect, but we have been asked to find friends who lay down their lives for us and to do the same for them. When you look around at your top five people, is there a mutual commitment to lay down your lives for one another? Does loving the people you surround yourself with now set you up to love those you are first called to care for? Does your commitment to this relationship bring out the best in both of you? Take just one step toward freedom by reevaluating the relationships closest to you.

Chapter 9
Building Boundaries

*I*f you grew up in small-town America, you know that everyone goes to the sporting events on Friday nights. During the junior high and high school years, our house was the hangout spot after school until the game began. It was basketball season, and some boys I knew from the opposing team decided to come by early. We had a houseful of teenagers, so I didn't notice the "joke" these boys had conjured up. One of the boys found a jar of pickles in our refrigerator, emptied the juice, and peed in the jar. He then put the jar right back in the fridge. (Gross!) You'll be happy to know that at least one of the boys' big mouths couldn't keep a secret. Before the basketball game even began, everyone knew what had happened. Luckily, I had friends who loved me enough to tell me, so no one fell victim to pee-pickles. Still, I was mortified.

On the way to the game, I told my mom what had happened. Let me tell you, hell hath no fury like a mother whose daughter has been embarrassed. My otherwise shy mother hunted one of those boys down during half-time and backed him right up into the corner near the concession stand where she was sure all the kids could bear witness. She told him, loudly, that she knew his dad, and that if he ever stepped foot into our house again, she would tell his dad and the police what he and his friends had done. I don't know whether it was the finger wagging in his face or the threat of the police, but the look of fear on his face was priceless! As a self-proclaimed "cool kid," I was embarrassed that my mom would tell this bully off in front of everyone. But behind my red face, I was relieved! I felt safe knowing that she loved me enough to stand up for me. I am pretty certain my mom didn't know that boy's dad, but by golly he believed her, and so did I. That boy didn't hang out around our town much after that. My mom had drawn a sharp line. She stood up to that jerk for me, she gave her expectations, and *boom!* Just like that, the bullying was over.

If you are a mother, I suspect you would do the same thing for your child. Why? Because you know your child has value and deserves to be treated with love and respect. But would you stand up for yourself? Do you love yourself enough to demand that you be treated with love and respect? If your answer is no, I hope you will remember that someone loves you and respects you enough to stand up for you. Identify that person or people in your life. Is it a friend, a sibling, parent, maybe even your child? Find someone who finds value in you and who has the courage to fight for you, then ask yourself how you can, for a brief moment, channel that courage to stand up for yourself. You've seen the WWJD (What would Jesus do?) bracelets; ask yourself WW_D. Fill in your letter. For me, it would be WWMD (What would Mom do?). Then I stand up for myself the way my mom would stand up for me. Once you have done this a time or two, you start realizing that you are, in fact, worthy to be fought for and valued. Eventually you might even be able to say WWID (What would I do?) because you value yourself enough to fight for what you need!

Setting new boundaries for my relationship with Carli wasn't easy. I couldn't just cut ties with her and be on my way. We lived in a small town and were bound to see each other at the local grocery store, and let's not forget we now worked together, which meant I had to interact with her. I also knew that Carli would fight dirty and tell anyone who would listen what a rotten person I was. I had shared secrets with her and allowed her to see my life up close, which meant she had seen all of my areas of weakness. From what I had witnessed, I knew it was very likely that she was sharing them with other people. At first, I considered beating her at her own game and telling my side of the story to everyone before she could. But part of cutting the ties of this toxic relationship meant that change had to start with me. I was determined to get out of this relationship while rebuilding my integrity. I refused to allow my past mistakes and slips in morals to define my future, so I started acting like the person I wanted to become.

As with the healing I'd experienced with my dad, the first step was prayer. I started with simple prayers, not big, beautiful, thought-out prayers—just tiny cries of my heart any time I felt the effects of the poison our relationship had left behind. In the shower, at the grocery store, while changing a diaper, I prayed, *God help please me. God, am I doing the right thing? God, if you love me, will you show me? God, how will I live without this friend? God, please give me my friend back.* I fought silently in front of others, but the battle in my soul was real, and the toxins sent shots of pain to my heart. During this time, I still maintained a relationship with Carli because I didn't know how to just abruptly stop being friends. I hoped our friendship could go back to how it was when it first started.

Matthew 18:15 (ESV) says, "If your brother sins against you, go and tell him his fault, between you and him alone. If he listens to you, you have gained your brother." I tried talking to Carli about how I felt. Each conversation left me hopeful and with a list of things I could do to make our friendship stronger, but I saw no changes in Carli.

God began answering my cries and delivering healing moments by placing people in my life whom I admired. Using the tips we talked about in the previous chapter, I found the courage to reach out to these new friends and invite them to do the things I had enjoyed doing with Carli. Instead of waiting for an invitation from someone else, I was the one inviting these new friends to concerts, to have coffee together, and to come hang out at the park. I realized that I needed to be the friend that I wanted in my life. I also knew that if I were looking for friends, other women must feel the same way. Soon I created an army of friends. I wasn't looking for people to share my stories about how bad it had been with Carli. I was looking for people who challenged me and made me feel stronger. Instead of looking for women who connected through gossip, I found women who focused on truth, ideas, and events that mattered. Philippians 4:8 (NIV) says, "Finally brothers and sisters, whatever is true, whatever is noble, whatever is right, whatever is pure, whatever is lovely, whatever is admirable—if anything is excellent or praiseworthy—think about such things." These new friends refreshed me like a cold drink of water. They were passionate about sharing ideas and dreams, not gossip and slander. When you are recovering from a toxic relationship, find people who are willing to lend you their confidence. You find your voice and strength when you spend time with smart women who live with integrity. Be sure that you are never the smartest person in your tribe of friends. Sure, you can be smarter

> **You find your voice and strength when you spend time with smart women who live with integrity.**

in one area or another, but when you look around, you all need to bring something important to the table to better one another.

I set basic boundaries, like finding new people to ride to work events with or not sharing important details of my life, which were easy to set in the beginning. When you are restructuring a relationship, it can be easy to fall back into old habits, so I never talked to Carli without a trusted friend nearby. I vowed to only correspond with her when it was absolutely necessary. My words would convey only facts and no details. Someone who isn't invested in my well-being does not have rights to the specifics of my life.

Resetting boundaries in toxic relationships can be difficult, particularly if your life is intertwined with the person, like mine was with Carli's. You can start with one set of boundaries and then readjust when you see that you are still emotionally influenced by your toxic friend. Like an addict quitting a physically addictive substance, there will be a period of discomfort as you learn to cleanse your mind from the lies you formed about you as a result of the relationship. Depending on how lethal the relationship was, your "friend's" jealousy over new friendships or anger about his or her sudden inability to control you may prompt a new kind of tension. Being aware will make all the difference. When you win an award, have an announcement of a baby, new home, milestone celebration, or beautiful vacation, you might suddenly start to hear from that person again. Be careful not to allow them to worm their way back into your life with the kindness that originally won you over.

Find someone in whom you can confide, someone who will help hold you accountable for keeping your boundaries in place. For me, this person was Rob. He had a front-row seat to the spectacle of my relationship with Carli. He had seen firsthand how it affected my emotions, and he could see how much stronger I was with my new boundaries in place. His encouragement served as the reminder I needed when I felt obligated to answer a call from Carli or would question why I had set the boundaries in the first place.

I second-guessed myself so many times while I was in that relationship. Later, I wondered what was wrong with me that I couldn't disconnect from her sooner. I've since discovered that relationships in which one person intentionally manipulates another's emotions are common. Even in the course of writing this book, I've coached several different women who feel trapped in relationships just like this one. These women are not immature, ignorant, or naive. As a matter of fact, they are smart, stable women who long for connection and love. They are ready and willing to care for and invest in people and would never use a friend for their own personal gain. They are smart enough to recognize manipulation techniques and unhealthy patterns in their relationships, but often because they are women who love big, they don't know how to break away from the dysfunction they have landed in.

No other time in history have people been so accessible. It is okay for you not to allow certain people to have 24/7 access into your life. In our social-media-driven world, the seemingly easiest way to set boundaries is by using the "unfriend" button. It's also the most annoying social media habit on earth (especially if you post about how lucky we all are that we didn't get "unfriended." Ummm . . . okay . . . thanks?). The unfriend button says, "I don't want you to see my kids, my new haircut, and certainly not what I'm having for dinner." Let's pause for a little social media lesson here: There are two ways to go about this: first is the "unfollow" or "mute" button, depending on which social media source you are using. Either button can be used without the other person knowing. You both still have full access to each other; you just don't see their posts in your newsfeed. I use this option when I see a post that kind of sends a little shock through my system that I call the "green jolt." The green jolt is a twinge of jealousy, irritation, or unnecessary emotion. It actually sends a little spark into your soul and prompts questions or statements like, "Why wasn't I invited?" or "Well, I could do that," or "She always seems to win," or "Why don't people like me enough to_____?" or "What the—" or "How dare she . . ." I hope you get the point here. Not all green jolts come from toxic relationships; often they come from your own insecurities or simply a bad day. But too many of those jolts can change how you feel about yourself, so unfollowing people is like your own personal negativity filter.

In toxic relationships, it's when something positive happens for you that the confrontation is most likely to occur. You buy a house, and she sends you an email telling you how lucky you are and how unlucky she is. You have a baby, and she calls while you're still in the hospital to talk about something "important" and subtly plants a seed of doubt about your ability to parent. You get a promotion, and she has an "emergency" and demands you take time off to help her with a project that just can't wait. There's nothing at all wrong with helping a friend who is in need, but when ulterior motives of manipulation become an obvious pattern, it's time to set (or adjust) your boundaries with that person and use the "unfriend" or "unfollow" button. The unfriend button ensures your "friend" cannot see anything you post that is marked for friends only.

In some cases, it may be necessary to "block" a person, which means they cannot even see that your account exists. Not only does this help you because your "accuser" can't see your posts, but it also takes away temptation to go look to see what they post because you can't see theirs either. Out of sight, out of mind! It may feel like a difficult decision to completely block someone because your own curiosity may make you wonder what they are up to. But in toxic relationships, blocking someone may be the first move toward standing up for yourself.

Outside of the virtual world, consider where you and your old friend might be connected. For Carli and me, it was the moms' groups, through friends, and through work. I had to switch things up, and that took courage. This is when I had to enlist that WWMD courage to fight for myself. It's also when I needed Rob to encourage me and remind me how my attitude and emotions affected other people when I ran into Carli with a mutual friend. For you, it may be that you need to start finding new friends who aren't connected to your ex-husband. Maybe it's as simple as asking a new coworker to lunch instead of going with the typical group. Maybe this year you do Thanksgiving with friends or a different side of the family while you establish your new boundaries. This step will be the hardest because it may require you to actually say no to your old friend, which is why it may also be the most important step you take. It may hurt to distance yourself from people you *do* like just to avoid someone you don't. But in giving yourself space, you aren't just avoiding someone you don't like, but you are also clearing away the obligation and guilt that hurtful person brings into your life. And each time you stand up for yourself, you become more like the person God created you to be.

Channel your champion's courage, and I promise peace and confidence will follow. If you don't have a champion standing in your corner, know this: I am here standing with you lending my confidence in you. You *can* do this, and you are worth fighting for. Feel free to ask yourself, *What would Lindsey do?* Here's my answer: I would stand up for you and tell you that this hard part is worth the struggle.

There will be phone calls that you will try to justify taking *because they are important.* There will be emails with subject lines that will be tempting to open, and there will be texts that you will want to read, but don't do it. This phase is temporary, but for a time period, you may need to cut all communication with that person.

Once you figure out where the toxic relationship disrupts your life the most, you can determine when and where to reestablish new boundaries. My guess is that you will find that you feel so confident and strong with those boundaries up that you won't want to adjust them.

It's important to communicate with the people around you who will be affected by your new boundaries. Be sure to proceed with caution. There is a fine line between gossiping and preserving your healthy relationships through constructive communication. You don't have to get into the dirty details; chances are, the people closest to you have already noticed the behavior and dysfunction of your relationship. Remember that the difference between gossip or complaining and problem-solving is who you tell and why you tell them. If the person you're talking to can't help you resolve the problem, you may just be venting. Venting seems harmless, but it isn't. When milk is spilled onto the floor, it doesn't just hit the initial spot of impact; it splatters in all different directions. It gets on things it never intended to touch. Your venting splatters onto everything it touches, potentially affecting all the areas around it. So if it's a coworker you need to set boundaries with, talk to your boss and let her know how not working with this person might improve your performance. Offer solutions and ask for help in creating boundaries that will have a minimal effect on the people around you. But keep the conversation between you and your boss. Not everyone you work with needs to be informed of the change. The truth is, people will notice even if you don't say a word.

If you and your sibling have a toxic relationship, talk to your other siblings or parents and let them know your intentions behind your actions. Let them know how hard it's been for you. Give them permission to stay out of any confrontations that may arise. (After all, they may have a completely healthy relationship with someone who is toxic for you.) As you consider who to tell and what to say, think about it like this: A piece of pineapple can be delicious and healthy to one person, and it can kill another person whose body reacts with an allergy. Someone with a pineapple allergy doesn't go around telling everyone that pineapples are unhealthy; that simply isn't true. Instead, they do their very best to avoid pineapple, double checking to be sure pineapple isn't in what they eat. They don't go checking everyone else's food. Your job in communicating with the people who will be affected by your new boundaries is to set the expectations regarding any changes in your behavior. In other words, you aren't eating pineapple anymore. Tell them you may not show up to Christmas this year. It doesn't have to be forever, but until the relationship has new and clear boundaries, big changes need to be made. Remember, you deserve this kind of peace in your life. You are loved, treasured, a child of the greatest King, who was and is, and is yet to come. I am standing next to you, holding your hand, helping you declare that you are worth it. Find your courage, make big, bold decisions, then find . . .

Silence.

Peace.

Stillness.

And then progress, betterment, growth.

Soon you'll ask why you took so long to set these boundaries. I am years on the other side of my toxic experience with Carli. It was a long journey, but now where there was insecurity, God has clothed me in His armor. Now when I see Carli, it is through much more confident eyes. I'm thankful for the friendship that helped me rediscover who I was in those early days when the relationship was healthy. I am also thankful for the person that struggle has transformed me into. I love that, through this journey, I realized how strong I am and that I am worth fighting for. The person you have a toxic relationship with likely has a history of repetitive behavior that looks much like the journey you had with them. Pray for them to find the kind of forgiveness and the courage to fight through fears that will make them feel whole again. Pray that one day, they will understand that they were made in the image of a great King and that they were meant to be loved. After all, they were made by the same Creator as you and I were, and they are worthy of the fight.

Chapter 10

Princess of Power—
Choose You!

I love a good accessory just as much as the next woman, but the number of hats most women wear in one day is something our moms could have never prepared us for. Taxi driver, soccer mom, world's best cookie maker, business woman, family financial expert, doctor, Victoria's Secret model wanna-be. One minute you are cleaning up dog poop off the kitchen floor, and the next you are a sex goddess to your husband. Forget about that drooling, fat-cheeked baby with a gummy smile in the next room. Seriously, you have to get him out of your mind, *concentrate,* because for the love of all things holy, you'd like to enjoy the hanky-panky too! *Oh, the pressure!*

Sure men take on many important roles, but women take on the world because we believe we can. Hats off to the men of the world who seem to know their limits. I don't have studies that prove this, but I am going to go out on a limb here and say that the princess story that stuck most with us as little girls was She-Ra: Princess of Power. *What*? You don't even know who she is? Well, let me tell you: She-Ra was a popular superhero in the 1980s. She-Ra wasn't just strong. According to Wikipedia, She-Ra is known for her incredible strength. Many times, she has been shown to be able to lift not only full-grown men and robots but also mountain-like rocks and buildings. She is also depicted as being extremely fast and acrobatic. Her speed allows her to easily deflect multiple incoming energy blasts with her sword. She-Ra also demonstrated a series of other abilities, which appear to be more nurturing in nature, such as empathic understanding, mental communication with animals, and healing. However, there is a limit to the length of time she can remain in her heroic form before she reverts to her original form.[1]

One day, I thought I could be just like She-Ra and use my super strength (in my pinky finger) to carry the milk from the car to the house. I made it into the house . . . but not to the kitchen. Just inside the front door, I dropped the milk, and it busted open all over the carpet. My mom was thrilled (said with great sarcasm). I am certain I didn't make it all the way to the kitchen with the milk because I was not allowed to wear my costume—which was actually She-Ra-themed Underoos. (I'm totally dating myself right now; if you don't know what Underoos are, then carry on.)

She was my hero!

The truth is, I am not, nor have I ever been, She-Ra. Neither are you. It's been years since I've outgrown those Underoos, but I still occasionally forget who I am and try to be She-Ra for a day, sometimes even for a week or months. I berate myself for being fully human and imperfect when I try to take on the world and fail.

I worry about things that I have no control over. I place unrealistic expectations on myself—expectations that would be impossible even for She-Ra to live up to.

Do you know what Wikipedia says about He-Man, She-Ra's male counterpart? He-Man was characterized as possessing super speed, indestructible skin, and *superhuman strength*.[2]

That's it.

He isn't trying to take on the world *and* be nurturing. He's laser focused on just a few superpowers.

She-Ra, on the other hand, has a list of things she's "super" at, but occasionally she unexpectedly reverts back to her original form. I wonder if she just gets tired.

Have you hit that season in your life yet, "She-Ra," when you yearn for your original form? Are you getting tired from trying to be super at everything?

Each time I transition into a new role, I feel a new set of expectations placed upon me. Isn't this why women ask the question, "What should I wear?" We don't want to show up in less than what is expected of us. Sometimes we've been given a list of expectations for our part, but more often, our expectations are an illusion that we have created. We set a rather lengthy list of rules and obligations that are unspoken, yet inflexible. Your duties and mine might be the same by title (i.e., mom, wife, daughter, sister, friend, business woman, teacher, etc.), but we each have our own set of criteria that makes us feel like we are doing "enough" in that role. The problem with our set of criteria is that we allow it to change with society or our season of life. When we start out as moms, we have ideas of what we'd like our parenting to look like. Then we start seeing how other people live and feed their families or which activities they sign up their kids for, and we change with the wind—adjusting our own expectations with those of everyone around us. Before long, we define motherhood as not just nurturing and caring for the people in our home but also volunteering for every opportunity to be our kids' coach or troop leader. I see it in businesswomen who have great momentum going in, then they begin adding systems and concepts because someone else shares an idea. The new tasks rarely create more energy. More often than not, they muck things up and slow down what was already working perfectly!

Ladies of the world, stop lying to yourselves about your obligations and expectations. It's time you know the truth about who you were created to be! No one except you expects you to flawlessly run the PTO, have a full-time job, keep a spotless home, put a healthy dinner on the table, get the kids to baseball practice, make it to the gym, get groceries, do your Bible study, read the kids a book before bed, and squeeze in time for intimacy too. If the list of areas you expect to be perfect at looks anything like that, it's likely you have dropped the ball big time on one or more occasion. And when you drop the ball, in creeps the guilt. You're feeding your family take-out regularly, you're not taking care of your body physically and mentally, you aren't being intimate with your husband, you don't have time to serve, and/or your house is beginning to resemble an episode of *Hoarders*. Likely, you're lying to yourself, expecting more than any one human can possibly handle alone, and feeling terrible about it in the process. The enemy wins when we believe the lie that we don't need help, and we have it all handled! Satan loves to make you shrink into a corner. He wants you to feel small and worthless—like a complete and utter failure. The best way to beat him at his game is to expose his lies and uncover the truth.

Lie #1: I rarely meet the expectations others set for me.

Truth: **Other people are way more forgiving of us than we are of ourselves.**

David Foster Wallace, who was called "one of the most influential and innovative writers of the last twenty years" by the *Los Angeles Times*, said, "You will become way less concerned with what other people think of you when you realize how seldom they do."[3] The first time I heard that quote, it came from my dad, and I heard it through those angry adolescent ears. I have since come to know and understand its truth. People simply don't think about us as much as we think about, worry about, and overanalyze ourselves. It's a reality that we all will disappoint people from time to time. It's unavoidable. Remember that most people don't have a front row seat to all the mistakes you make. And the truth is, when you start saying no to some obligations that don't align with their values and priorities, they might get annoyed.

Your responsibility, however, is not to keep other people happy. It is to focus on the people who matter most in your life. Do that, and everything else will become clear in terms of what you "should" or "should not" be doing, managing, or volunteering for. If you find it necessary to justify why you are bowing out of certain areas or not adopting new practices with other people—in hopes that they will understand you better—realize you will spend a significant part of your life explaining yourself. Don't spend more than three minutes thinking, worrying, or talking about it if it won't matter in three years. I hope you hear my heart here: We should also be serving those outside our homes, as there are times when systems need to be changed up or new ideas need to be implemented. There will always be great opportunities for you to invest your time and energy in something new. But before you act out of fear, guilt, or obligation, step back and consider if the opportunity of the moment is the one that needs you most. Will you be able to implement this new change, commitment, or opportunity without sacrificing what's most important to you?

Proverbs 10:28 (ESV) reminds us, "The hope of the righteous brings joy, but the expectation of the wicked will perish."

Lie #2: The more I do, the more I'm worth.

Truth: **If you do nothing today except breathe in and out, you are worthy of love.**

At a recent Bible study I attended, we considered this question: If God asked you why He should allow you into heaven, what would your answer be? People immediately began listing things like good attributes, volunteering, being kind to others, serving the homeless, sacrificing, tithing. You name it; we found good works in ourselves. It was a trick question because you can do nothing to earn your way into heaven. Your worth is not about what you've done, but it is about what has been done for you on the cross through Jesus Christ. This is a hard truth to wrap our brains around, no matter if you've been a Christian your whole life or one week. Simply put, we have been trained in school, in work, and even at home that if we work hard, we get rewards. But that is the human way, not God's way.

> If you do nothing today except breathe in and out, you are worthy of love.

If you show up for what matters most, God will bless your work. That doesn't mean that you are more likely to get into heaven. Ten years ago if you had asked me what I would be doing today, I would have given you one hundred different scenarios, none of which would have included running a successful direct-selling business. I certainly wouldn't have told you that I would have five children or would be writing a book. Some of the work I have been called to do through the years has been hard, even heartbreaking. Some of it has been fun and exciting. But in every instance when I chose to not do the hardest thing but the next right thing, my work felt rewarding and was covered in teachable moments. I simply showed up, and God blessed the path through joy and through struggle because I was obedient—not because I did more than anyone else or was flawless in my efforts. Take one step forward, and He will carry you a mile. Take another step forward, and He will lead you to the peak of a mountain. Even steps backward, sideways, or those that land you flat on your face seem to lead to the rewarded path created just for you.

Doing more (and more and more) in an effort to try to control our lives drowns out the voice of God and sends the message that we don't trust the pathway He has created for us. Don't mishear what I am saying. I get overly frustrated with people who say, "If God wants it to be, it will happen." That's not how it works. God created you to take action. You cannot pray for a lean, healthy body and never show up at the gym or eat a single vegetable to get it. But when the control causes angst or feelings of inadequacies, our job isn't to do more or try harder. Our job is to show up every day with God's plan to grow us in mind. We need to bring faith the size of a mustard seed (Matthew 17:20) and watch God work miracles through us, strengthen us, and grow our faith.

After all, Ephesians 2:8–9 (NIV) states, "For it is by grace you have been saved, through

> **Our job isn't to do more or try harder. Our job is to show up every day with God's plan to grow us in mind.**

faith—and this is not from yourselves, it is the gift of God—not by works, so that no one can boast."

Lie #3: I can please others by going along with the crowd.

Truth: **You do you. Watch the people around you come alive in their own individuality!**

Compromising who you are to make others happy will lead you down a broken road. Maybe you have been following along for so long that you don't know exactly who you are. That means it's time to search for your core values, the truths you hold most dear. They affect and are integrated into your faith, financial security, family, education, philanthropy, and success. They define how you want to be perceived. Be careful here because these values can be manipulated and manifest in unhealthy ways; for example, you can be budget conscious for the betterment of your family, but there is a fine line between budget conscious and greed. You may value education and surround yourself with friends who do the same. But if your children's homework and studies become more important than attending a weeknight Bible study group, things might be out of alignment with your value of faith. Our core values need to be balanced and checked frequently, otherwise we risk allowing an asset to turn into a hindrance.

Sometimes we are moving along well, and our core values shift because of the people we spend time with. Maybe they don't attend church weekly, or they are okay with racking up credit card bills, or maybe they spend more time than we would training for marathons, and we join in. What can it hurt to miss a Sunday or invest more time into our fitness? But by letting go of our own core values and clinging to someone else's, we give away a little of our integrity. Remember the children's Sunday school song, "The wise man built his house upon the rock"? We all know what happened to the foolish man's house built on the sand, right? It went "splat." Every time I build my house upon the sand of someone else's values, my house begins to crumble.

Women are especially vulnerable to going along with the crowd. You say yes to one more drink when you know you shouldn't. You buy the sweater that is not in your budget because your friends tell you how great you look. Add the bonus that now all your friends think you're gorgeous . . . *budget smudget*! Who cares about getting out of debt? Everyone else is in debt too! Your best friend really needs your help. After all, no one else is properly suited to take on the big school festival task all on their own. So you say yes when you really want to say no—and you compromise the family time you cherish most.

Whatever the compromise is, you rationalize it away. It's not like you are saying yes to snorting a line of cocaine. But the truth is that these little bitty yeses eat away at your energy and take you from the things you treasure most. Even a task that seems noble can pull you from the work God has called you to do and the person He has created you to be.

You don't have to be liked by everyone. (*Gulp.*) That's a hard pill to swallow! I struggle with this one big time. Maybe you've heard that you can be the most beautiful, round, juiciest peach in the world, and there will be someone who doesn't like peaches. You can't know this fact and then go on and try to make everyone like you anyway. Even Jesus Christ was not loved by everyone. John 16:33 (NIV) reminds us, "I have told you these things, so that in me you may have peace. In this world you will have trouble. But take heart! I have overcome the world." Find your peace in knowing that you are loved and created for a purpose. That purpose and love does not depend on what others think of you but rather how your Creator made you.

Lie #4: I have to give 100 percent to my children and husband at all times.

Truth: **Teaching your children and husband to operate without you is your gift—to them and to yourself.**

Make no mistake: Your most primary obligations lie with the people who live in your four walls. There may be a few people you have obligations with outside of those walls, but your family will always be your first calling over any other opportunity that presents itself. What is it that *they* need and expect from you?

In recently years, my work has required more travel. With five kids, that means missed sporting events and even an occasional missed birthday. I felt such immense pressure to be there for 100 percent of the games and, of course, never miss a birthday, but missing some of these events would have affected our financial security. After I spent days wallowing in my worry about what to do, I decided to ask them what they expected. I explained that I needed to travel for work and that I needed their input on what I should do. Their expectations of me were much lower than mine of myself. They hoped I would make it to 80 percent of their games. They said that if an 80 percent was a good grade on a test that it should be a good grade as a parent. What a huge relief!

I don't have to give 100 percent to everything I do, and neither do you. I know this isn't what you are used to hearing. We like to give it 100 percent all the time, but the math doesn't work out. Decide with the people who you are called to first what you can do. Set clear standards. For me, I know I can show up to 80 percent of school activities 100 percent of the time. To help relieve even more pressure, my kids told me they thought it was more important that they had a birthday celebration than that the celebration was held on the day of their birthday. As they get older, they really just want me to fork over the birthday card filled with cash anyway! I wonder how many of these wrinkles I could have held off for a few years had I just asked the question when it first plagued me. Not only did they have lesser expectations of me than I had of myself, but my family felt valued because I included them in this big decision. No more guessing games!

In a business where many of the women are, like I was, stay-at-home moms looking to add to their income, fathers are not often left to be the main caretaker of their children. This becomes an issue for women wanting to go to learning retreats and conferences. They will stress themselves out the week prior to their two days away creating lists, making meals, and writing love notes to their children for each day they are gone. They cover all of the tasks, carpools, meals and more, worried that their husbands need them to be there 100 percent of the time to help things run smoothly. Newsflash, ladies—your man is way more capable than you are giving him credit for or than he is letting on. Allow your husband to plan, prepare, feed, and veg out with the kids. Will he do it like you? No! Will the house be a mess when you get home? Maybe. Will they eat junk all weekend? Probably! But he will do it like a dad, which will show them how capable he is, how invested he is, and it will remind them that Mom trusts Dad. It will remind them that Mom deserves some time to herself and that the world does not cave in when Mom goes out of town. Furthermore, it's okay for the kids to have a break from their daily routine too. Empower your husband to be their dad, and let yourself off the hook this time. They will be okay without you!

Think about how much easier relationships with our spouses, siblings, and friends will be if we ask them questions about what they need and empower them to be who they are. Honey, what do you need for me to do tonight? How do you like me to tell you when I am upset with you? What can I do to take stress off you when you feel overwhelmed? What about statements like: "Oh,

Dad's got everything under control! He can handle it," or "Honey, you and the kids will have a great time. There's frozen pizzas in the freezer!"

What an incredible team we can make with the people around us if we simply ask the important questions and allow the people around us to step up when we need to step out! Psalm 29:11 (ESV) says, "May the LORD give strength to his people! May the LORD bless his people with peace!"

Lie #5: I'm failing.

Truth: **You are a work in progress.**

Have you actually set standards for yourself? I know you have expectations that change with what society asks of you, but I'm talking about written-down rules of what makes you a successful candidate to be you. When I think of setting expectations for someone, I think of a job description. Make a job description, including tasks and characteristics you expect from yourself. Read the description back and ask yourself if you would apply for that job. If the answer is no, go through and see where you can delete tasks or, better yet, add time in for celebration for all that you accomplish!

Be aware, though, you weren't made to be perfect and fill all voids. Certain seasons may require you to have a shorter job description than others. Keep the perspective that even slow progress is progress, and a setback isn't a failure. Keep moving forward, sister—you are a work in progress!

Remember, the new you isn't going to try to be the perfect wife/mom/business owner/volunteer/chef/caretaker *all* of the time. Just show up, give what you have to give, and trust that God will multiply your efforts when you are faithful to Him. Even as you give and grow, keep in mind that who you are to God has nothing to do with how good a wife/mom/business owner/volunteer/chef/caretaker you are. In other words, stop trying to earn God's grace and love. It's already yours—if you are willing to accept it.

Think of what it means to be given a grace period in the financial world. It's a pause, a place where nothing is expected of you, a penalty-free zone. Jesus gives you grace all the time. Extend that same grace to yourself. As long as you are giving yourself grace to be imperfect, but not permission to quit on yourself, you are still a work in progress. Set clear standards for yourself and stop adjusting the bar every time someone tells you how high to jump. Create a mission for your life and try to look at that mission or job description from an outside view. If you were reading that job description as *someone else's* personal expectations for herself, would you tell her it was realistic—or impossible to live up to? Show up, set reasonable, faith-filled standards, and pray for God to bless the vision you've asked for in your life. If that vision makes you stronger in your faith and closer to your core values and your family, you'll soon be watching your heart's desires come alive.

> **Even slow progress is progress, and a setback isn't a failure. Keep moving forward, sister—you are a work in progress!**

As Jeremiah 33:3 (ESV) states, "Call to me and I will answer you and will tell you great and hidden things that you have to me and I will answer you and will tell you great and hidden things that you have not known."

Chapter 11

Grace Over Guilt

*J*ohn 12:27a (NIV) states, "Now my soul is troubled, and what shall I say? 'Father, save me from this hour'?"

Confession time: I am hiding in my bedroom from my kids. Don't judge me! It is utter chaos around here. I have five kids, three dogs, and a cat. I know what you're thinking, and I am aware what caused the five kids. And I may have let those five kids convince me we needed at least three of the animals. I'm a sucker for something cute and cuddly.

Reading and writing feed my soul, so while I hide, I write and decompress. I fill my own cup that has been depleted by the mayhem I chose and love but from which I occasionally need a break. Kids, work, and life pull me in a million directions every day. A quiet hour in my bedroom hiding, reading, and writing makes me happy. I used to feel lousy about that, but now I know it's a necessary part of my day.

Usually, just as I settle into my big, comfy writing chair, my youngest daughter finds me and asks in her sweet voice, "Mommy, do you want to play dolls with me?" I know it's been days (who am I kidding, weeks) since I actually sat and played with her one-on-one. The truth is, I have no desire to play imaginary games. If that didn't make you cringe, maybe this will: Not only do I not like to play "pretend" with my kids, but I don't feel one bit guilty about it.

I spent years feeling guilty about who I am as a mother, or maybe I should I say who I am not. I gave that up when I realized guilt was only depleting my energy and making me a terrible mom, wife, and friend. Each of us only has a limited supply of energy, and spending energy on guilt wears you down. It drives you to walk around all day feeling like you are not enough, or maybe you feel guilty because you think you are too much. You long to be great for those who need you the most—your parents, friends, husband, children—but guilt suffocates the beating of your heart. It pulls you in directions you never meant to go and leaves you running on fumes for those you most want to serve. It's that heavy blanket of FOG I have mentioned so many times before, too much to carry but too heavy to put down.

Over the years, I have coached full-time moms, part-time working moms, full-time working moms, and even moms who work from home full time. Not only have I coached them, but I have lived each of those seasons of life. Mommy guilt is inescapable! "Do my kids think the world revolves around them?" "Do my kids not see me enough?" "Do my kids like the nanny more than they like me?" "Am I ruining my kids because I am on the computer when they are here?" Should I go on?

In pops that necessary evil for most of us, social media, and it's a recipe for the best guilt sandwich life has to offer! Facebook, Pinterest, Instagram—no matter which poison you pick, it only takes the click of a button to see the amazing day all of your friends have had. Meanwhile, you feel like all you've done today is break up fights, wipe boogers out of noses, and you're fairly certain, because of the smell, you may have forgotten deodorant. Maybe you're on the opposite end where you haven't seen your kids all day, and you miss them terribly.

Have you ever decided to see a movie after watching an awesome movie trailer and then been disappointed because all the good parts were in the trailer? Social media is the trailer of each person's life. We sit on our side of the computer watching all our friends' movie trailers; meanwhile, we are living in our own full-length picture. We see all of our faults and wonder why we didn't make a real dinner tonight instead of going out to the fast food joint again. We wonder why we don't like to play board games with our kids. We assume that the girl down the street wakes up looking that beautiful and put together. We start questioning our performance, our efforts, and when we got that wrinkle in between our eyebrows. We have to stop comparing our full motion picture to other people's movie trailers. Comparison not only tries to threaten those expectations we have worked hard to set for ourselves, but it also steals our joy. Social media has a great place in our culture. I love how it has connected loves, friendships, and relatives, but it is also a feasting ground for Satan. He loves to tell you lies while you are scrolling through those pages. The enemy loves to remind you of how unworthy you are of love from others because you have gained a few pounds. He loves to make you feel not good enough, not included, and more than anything he wants you to believe that you are capable of being all things to all people. If he can keep you focused on those lies, you will run yourself ragged—and you won't have a single minute left in your day to connect with God, who will whisper truths in your heart.

If you take a giant step back and look at your life from the outside, you may see either 1) a woman who is kept so busy by guilt that she's afraid to stop, for fear that she won't get back up, or 2) a woman who is so tired and bogged down by the guilt that she has given up and hidden herself under layers of fat or laziness that indicate she has surrendered to the guilt. Whichever category you fall under, it's time to open your eyes to your own highlight reel and start living the majority of your time in it! No more lies telling you that you can be all things to all people. No more lies telling you that you aren't enough to get out and get the job done. Now is the time! If you want to wake up a year from now living a life different than the one you are living today, you will have to start making small changes right now. There is no need for a new year or new day to create that change. Make a decision and determine what actions are necessary to make it happen.

Begin by praying about whatever part of your life is plagued with guilt. "Lord, if you called me to this journey, why do I feel like I am failing at it? Help me feel like I am enough." It is okay for you to question God. Recognize that condemnation comes from the enemy and conviction comes from Jesus Christ. Condemnation gives you that feeling in the pit of your stomach saying you aren't enough; you'll never be able to handle this. It's the green jolt reminding you of your extra forty pounds when your friend posts her successful before and after photos. It holds you captive, telling you you'll never have success like your sister has at her business. It lies and says they don't like you because you weren't invited to the girls' night out. Conviction is from God; it may create sorrow or even that short thought of "I'm sick of where I am," but it promotes movement and calls you into

> Conviction is from God; it may create sorrow or even that short thought of "I'm sick of where I am," but it promotes movement and calls you into action; it shows you ways around obstacles.

action; it shows you ways around obstacles. Conviction will prompt you to plan your own girls' night out with women you don't know well yet. It's gives you the courage to not just start your own successful business but to stick with it this time. It will motivate you to create a plan to successful weight loss. Conviction urges you to step outside of your comfort zone and try that new hobby. Often conviction will prompt you to take actions that you could never take alone. If you're ever wondering what God's voice sounds like, that's it! It causes you to move forward when you otherwise would have sat in your pity.

I hate playing dolls or ninjas or dolls who are ninjas who run a library (I told you my kids were crazy.), but does that alone define the kind of parent I am? I made a list of things I love to do with my kids. The list included, but wasn't limited to, brushing hair, watching movies, painting nails, reading, praying, volleyball, basketball, playing board games, and if I'm feeling extra competitive, I might even play a video game. But when it comes to me pretending to be a doll in some imaginary world or pretending to crash or blow something up, I left those items off the list.

In order to evaluate whether my mommy guilt was condemnation or conviction, I asked myself if I was sinning by not wanting to play "make-believe" with my kids. I wasn't feeling lust, anger, greed, or jealousy. I wasn't gossiping, slandering, lying, or swearing (even though I want to while I play dolls). I wasn't sinning by not wanting to make the time to handmake my children's Halloween costumes like so many of my creative friends on Facebook do. Satan was condemning me, making me feel guilt and a sense of unworthiness, and frankly, I was done letting his lies run my confidence dry. I love my children. I wake up every day and make nearly every choice with them in mind. Sometimes that means that I *need* to lock myself in a room, go to the gym, get my nails done, or have a glass of wine with a friend, even though I worked all week—to make money—*for them.*

Placing value on making time for what you need is not just okay; it is healthy. If I show up to play dolls with my kids and I am not enjoying it, they feel that disconnect—mostly because I then keep my phone near me and check it every five minutes or fall asleep on the floor. Neither of us feels like we want to be there when I am only partially engaged. When I look at my seven-year-old daughter and say, "Paige, I am taking some time for me right now. How about right after dinner we play a game of Connect Four?" she learns that she can grow to value herself too. She learns that while she is important, the world doesn't revolve around her. Although I will say the "world revolving around her" message, she may not have fully grasped it yet. We're working on it!

Leadership and self-development books and trainings are filled with time-management tools that I have found to be useless. The most successful people I know aren't great time managers, rather they are great *energy* managers. I can spend the exact same amount of time playing volleyball with my kids as I can playing dolls, and when I am finished, I will feel completely different. One activity sucks the life out of me, and the other recharges me and gives me the energy to spend my evening pouring into my marriage, my job, or even my housework (Sorry, ladies, some obligations are unavoidable.) Get intentional about your energy. Don't just grab what comes your way in life. Plan the moments you want to grab. Create moments that fill you with energy to carry you through your day. The more energy you have, the more time you will find, because you are full and invigorated.

I asked some friends what the one thing was they felt most guilty about in life, and almost every one of them said their lack of intimacy with their husbands. When I asked them why they think that's an issue, they said they just had no energy left! One woman even told me that lack of intimacy was the one and only reason her marriage ended. There is no doubt that the lack of sex in marriage can cause some regret and guilt, so before we end this chapter, we need to have a serious talk about why putting energy into the physical part of your marriage is essential. Putting your marriage relationship at the top of your list of priorities will change every dynamic in your home. Trust me on this. Do not let the millions of things or little people on your schedule steal this joy for you. If you think back to before the little people came along, I know you remember a time when it's all you wanted to do! A healthy sex life in a marriage will add energy to your home, create open communication between parents, and in turn, increase the joy in your days.

Plan a weekly date night—to the movies, to get groceries, to sit in your backyard and eat pizza. It doesn't matter what you do, but do it together! No kids allowed! I know what you're thinking: It's expensive, babysitters and nights on the town, but you know what else is expensive? Divorce! It costs money, time, and it drains your children's trust accounts. Not only that, but God intended for marriage to be the earthly picture of how he feels about his church. Satan has so much to win if you don't feel confident in your marriage. Feel too fat for sex? Satan wins. Feel too tired for sex? The enemy takes over. Too angry for intimate conversations? Score one for the bad guy. You need to think of intimacy with your husband as his way of communicating with you. How would you feel if he never talked to you because he was just too tired? That's how he feels when you say "not tonight" every night because you are just too tired. Men were made to be sexual and to communicate intimacy without words. If your marriage is in a place where you are communicating very little and you are blaming that for your lack of desire for intimacy, realize that the two often go hand-in-hand. Have sex, he talks, talk, she has sex. Someone has to give in first!

If physical intimacy is an area of your life that is lacking, it's one that I would put at the top of your job description. One day, those precious babies are going to leave your home, and you're going to be left spending the majority of your life alone with a man you haven't been intimate with in twenty years. Make your marriage relationship a priority!

Society tries to make divorce look like a convenient option, an easy way out. But it never is. Divorce, even the "amicable" ones, create casualties. Decide for you and your family that divorce is not an option. I understand that your sweet children are cuter than your husband and his balled-up socks on the floor, but if you want to take care of your kids, take care of your marriage first. I do understand that there are some circumstances for which this doesn't apply. I am talking about a marriage where two people are living as roommates and setting each other's needs aside for the betterment of the children. If there are psychological or physical reasons for a lack of sex or connection in your home, please seek professional help in working through those issues; if your husband isn't willing to go with you, go alone! You can only control you.

Now that you have learned to identify what is causing your fears, obligations, and guilt, you should easily begin wiping out anything that drains your energy. At first, making time and mental space for physical intimacy will be difficult. Satan will try to swoop in and cloud up your schedule with all kinds of obligations, maybe even some arguments and bigger reasons why not to connect physically. Keep your job description in mind and put date night on the calendar first every week. Work every other commitment around it. You may be reading things and thinking, *My marriage is great!* That's wonderful! Keep working on it. Noah spent more than one hundred years building the ark before the flood came! Building a strong relationship that can last through life's storms starts now. Be intentional about connecting with your husband. You, your husband, and your kids deserve it.

When Satan tries to condemn or suppress your worth, when he lies to you about who you are and what you have time for, remember you were created for connection. You were created for relationship, in the likeness of God. You were created with a specific set of skills and gifts. As you lean into the works and gifts you were created for, you will start to see things more clearly. You will see your life become this beautiful, fulfilling tapestry woven by God—using your hands. Listen for the convictions of the Holy Spirit to remind you that you are worthy, you are capable, and you are loved.

Chapter 12

When Opportunity Knocks ... Ask for Identification

There is a big difference between being called and being capable. It's easy to look at a calendar or a skill and say, "I can do that," but when it comes down to it, is that trip or project really for you?

As a new Christian, I started listening to Contemporary Christian music on the radio. I loved it, but I always changed the station before I got out of the car so Rob wouldn't know my secret appreciation for the "safe for the whole family" station. Then one day, a passing comment at a work conference changed everything. I was chatting with the women in line near the bathrooms. We were making small talk with those we didn't know well. The conversation went to popular country music artists. One lady I had admired from her training on stage earlier that day said, "I have no idea who y'all are talkin' about." Surprised, I asked, "Well, what kind of music do you listen to?" Matter-of-factly she said, "I listen to Christian music." That one sentence changed my life. Sounds silly, right? But her profession of love for my kind of music validated my music choice in my mind. I began leaving the Christian station on when I got out of the car. I began noticing that after Rob took the car, the station was still on. Now our entire family shares a love for Christian music. We start each morning with songs of praise and joy, which sets the tone for our day. Now these are not hymns, which are perfectly fine but not the music I'm talking about. These are contemporary, fun-to-listen-to songs that we dance and sing to just like we would any other popular song. But in these songs, there are fewer (as in no) lyrics about booty shorts and drinking. The one comment from a woman I admired moved the needle and made an impact on the lives of seven people. Now my kids can be caught humming a tune to a song that portrays truth about their worth. God planned that moment in line at the bathrooms. That job was created just for the woman I had admired on that stage that day. Had another woman said the same sentence, it may not have had the same impact. If she would have planned it, it would have been awkward and ineffective. If the words had come from another woman in the conversation, they would have come and gone without being remembered. But now my children have tunes of truth etched into their minds and hearts. As adults, these will be the tunes of their childhood that they share with the next generation.

There is no such thing as a small assignment. Things like volunteering to be a Sunday school teacher or hosting the bridal shower or committing to a weekend of travel seems like an insignificant endeavor but can leave impact that lasts a lifetime. You may never even know which moments God chooses from your life to impact another person. The moments you think you have some grand assignment will result in little, and moments you don't even remember will move someone's heart forever. Think about moments or single sentences that have been spoken to you that shaped your heart or even just changed the trajectory of your day. You've had moments that shift a day and some that have altered your life's course. If you have ever told someone who was part of that change how they impacted your life, usually they receive the news with surprise. It seems as though God delights in using seemingly insignificant moments or chance meetings to make the biggest difference.

The opportunities created for *you* are so important! Don't miss them by saying yes to an opportunity created for someone else. You'll easily recognize when you have said yes to someone else's opportunity because it becomes your burden. Ephesians 2:10 (NLT) says, "For we are God's masterpiece. He has created us anew in Christ Jesus, so we can do the good things he planned for us long ago." If that woman, who is now a dear friend, had said yes to another job opportunity, had said no to presenting on stage that day, or had walked to a different bathroom line, seven lives would have been here, but seven mornings may have never started with encouragement and truth each morning before school. Countless moments of being moved to tears hearing my son and

> **You'll easily recognize when you have said yes to someone else's opportunity because it becomes your burden.**

daughter singing along with the truths in these songs would have gone unshed. Our first family concert may have never happened because our family might never have connected through this music. But they did—because of one simple, seemingly insignificant moment in the ladies' room. One of my favorite authors Andy Andrews says it best in his book, *The Butterfly Effect*, when he says, "Every action or inaction you make matters."

You'll know that you've obligated yourself to an assignment not made for you when you start to dread it. Obligations will exhaust you mentally, physically, and emotionally. You may show up for the moment, but when your heart isn't in it, it diminishes the experience for everyone. When my oldest son was in kindergarten, I signed up to be a room parent. Honestly, I heard it was hard to get the position because so many moms were willing. So when I was chosen, I was thrilled! I thought it would entail spending time with my son and getting to know his friends. Instead, I felt like I was herding adults and begging people to help at classroom parties. I didn't show up to meetings with fun ideas or care which craft or game was played because I wasn't interested in coordinating the games; I just wanted to show up and play with the kids. If you are a room mother, please know that I love you. I value what you add to children's classrooms everywhere. I realized early on that I was capable of being the room mom. Anyone can show up and do what I did, but I wasn't adding an extra touch of passion to it. When your heart and your mind connect on a project, no matter how big or small, you'll recognize it by the energy it brings to your day. The time will fly by and you won't be able to stop thinking about the next time you can be part of that activity again. More importantly, regardless of whether you are filing paperwork, teaching children, or singing in front of thousands, you will see God's hand in the work that was created just for you.

Don't expect your calling to always be comfortable. As I sit and type this, I am reminded that we aren't always called to the thing we are most comfortable with, but we will always be called to the area where we can make the greatest impact for God. You'll learn to lean on God more than ever to accomplish the work He has prepared for you. It's why I put this chapter after the one preparing you to clean out and rebuild your relationships. You'll need to be surrounded by godly people who lift you to accomplish the work that God has prepared for your life. You'll need people who won't allow you to quit when your calling gets tough. You'll need people who believe in you.

> We aren't always called to the thing we are most comfortable with, but we will always be called to the area where we can make the greatest impact for God.

While many people like to make pros and cons lists before they decide to take on something new, I find those lists to be ineffective. The problem is that not every item on the list weighs the same. For example, your family time would weigh more than something that simply makes you feel good. Instead, as I have encouraged over and over, pray about every opportunity that comes across your email and text. In every piece of work that someone thinks you'd be great for, ask God if it was meant for you. He will often answer quickly because he cares about the details of your life. Luke 12:7 (NIV) says, "Indeed, the very hairs of your head are all numbered. Don't be afraid; you are worth more than many sparrows."

Every opportunity we accept requires a no to something we once considered a yes. Jobs not created for you feel rushed, have a sense of urgency behind them, or may leave you feeling uneasy. Your job may have a quick timeline, but it will always come with

> **If God made an opportunity for you, He will keep it for you.**

an underlying sense of peace and excitement. Someone else's job leaves you feeling like you have to grab the opportunity fast before it slips through your fingers. If God made an opportunity for you, He will keep it for you. If it doesn't align with your life's priorities or core values, it's easier to say no.

I've watched enough *Deadliest Catch* to know that a ship has an enclosed area called a wheelhouse. There must always be a captain in the wheelhouse. The captain's main jobs are to steer the boat, to keep the crew safe, and to decide where to drop the "pods" for crab. (I know this is simplified immensely, but stick with me.) The captain cannot go out on the deck and pull in the pods full of crab or make dinner for the crew. He has specific duties inside his wheelhouse. To keep the ship and its crew safe, he has to stay in the wheelhouse.

What is inside of your wheelhouse? Where do you need to focus to keep your boat moving toward the goal? For me, it's nurturing my faith, feeding my family both physically and emotionally, and self-care. When you look at your own wheelhouse, you may find that some of your current commitments don't fit. Bow out of those obligations respectfully. Identifying what's in your wheelhouse is a way to narrow down your life's job description and keep you focused on the healthy expectations you've set for yourself.

When you use the right words to say no, people will be supportive and understanding. Say things like: "Thank you for inviting me to be a room parent; I really feel like I'm better suited to come and help at the party so I can spend time with my kids." "I'm so honored you would think of me, but right now I have some other priorities I am focusing on." "Thanks for asking me to donate, but all of our resources are accounted for right now." If you have already committed to something and you realize it doesn't fit into your wheelhouse, try saying, "After giving this a try for a little bit, I realized that I may have said yes to too many activities. I am planning to finish (Insert anything you need to wrap up.), but then I'm going to refocus on some priorities in my life." You will start to feel lighter and realize that when you clear your schedule for what matters most to you, you will accomplish things you never knew possible. Most people spend eight hours a day building someone else's dream and then come home to fulfill obligations for others. If that's your situation, it's no wonder that you may feel tired and stretched thin! It's time to focus on *your* opportunities and watch your dreams unfold in front of your eyes.

Chapter 13

Forgiving Your Way to Transformation

"*But the LORD said to Samuel, 'Do not look on his appearance or on the height of his stature, because I have rejected him. For the LORD sees not as man sees: man looks on the outward appearance, but the LORD looks on the heart'*" (1 Samuel 16:17 ESV).

Have you ever had a spray tan? Not like on the episode of *Friends* where the machine tells Ross what to do, and he fails miserably. I'm talking about the kind where the technician actually physically sprays your body. If you haven't, you must have beautiful olive skin that turns a gorgeous color of golden brown in the sun. For me, it's either slathering myself in SPF 100 or ending a week at the beach a shade of lobster. Often I like to get a nice spray tan when I'm going on a vacation. It just makes me feel better about myself! The experience begins with you standing totally naked while another human gets about six inches from your body and sprays you all over with a light mist. It's cold and uncomfortable, but the results are a glowing, beautiful, sun-kissed body, and I am not above the humiliation for a little beauty.

Imagine having nursed five children and standing buck naked, waiting on your spray-tan technician. Every single physical imperfection is not just on parade, but there is a full-length mirror so you can see the process. For my first spray tan, my technician was a Greek goddess. She was a gorgeous young lady who came into the room wearing what appeared to be a pair of jeans from the size zero rack. Her perfectly wavy hair cascaded down her back and was the shiniest color of golden brown I had ever seen. Add to that her flawless skin, barely covered in any makeup, and I wasn't intimidated at all. Nope. Not one bit.

I had been in this situation before, you know, in those nightmares when you go back to high school and forget to wear clothes. We all know how that ends up. (Actually I don't because I always wake up sweating before I get to the end.) I digress. There I was, naked as a jaybird, and standing in front of this gorgeous woman. *I bet she just thinks I am gross*, I thought. Which made me decide in an instant that I didn't like her. I created a story of what she probably was thinking about me. It went something like this: *I feel so sorry for this poor, fat woman. Life must be horrible to wake up and see that you have a round belly and stretch marks all over. I feel even more sorry for her husband who has to look at this every day. I wonder if she knows if she just eats clean and exercises more, she could look more like me.* All of my insecurities were running circles in my brain. My past decisions haunted me. I suddenly regretted choosing wine over the water, the brownie over the apple, and sleeping in over going to the gym. The aversion I felt toward her was charged by the shame of all those little choices I'd made over time.

I did the only thing I knew to do; I made small talk. Our conversation quickly turned to family. When I'm nervous, I talk a lot, so I went on and on about my husband and all my kids for a while before asking her about her life. She was thirty-three and had been married for ten years. She and her husband were unable to have children. Immediately I felt ashamed of myself for being so embarrassed of my child-marked body and my mom haircut. A new perspective made me wonder if I could hear her thoughts, would they have sounded like this: *I wonder if Lindsey feels sorry for me. I wonder what it would be like to wake up with a beautiful round belly and stretch marks not just once, but five times. I bet Lindsey's husband is so proud to wake up to all those kids each day. I wonder if she knows that I exercise to keep busy and eat clean to try to get my body to work perfectly to make and nourish a baby.* I will never know the thoughts of my beautiful technician, but now when I meet someone, I try to remember that there is a story being woven in her heart too. No matter how put together she looks, she has struggles, and she has had to bump heads with her own reality.

Jesus's half-brother James says in James 1:2–3 (NIV): "Consider it pure joy, my brothers and sisters, whenever you face trials of many kinds, because you know that the testing of your faith produces perseverance." Hard times are the richest soil for growth. As the saying goes, everyone we meet is fighting a battle we know nothing about. The most responsible use of the gift of grace is to be curious enough about other people to pay it forward. Jesus has given me the gift of grace because He knows me. He knows all the good and all the nasty in my heart, and He even knows things about me that I don't. I, however, don't have that knowledge or access to the people who I cross paths with daily. My quest is to find out as much as I can about people! I love to curiously ask questions of how they came to their current situation.

> **Hard times are the richest soil for growth.**

Do you ever find yourself standing in a room full of people, feeling uncomfortable with no one to talk to? Maybe you're at a company event, standing next to someone with whom you assume you have nothing in common. Ask bigger questions than "How are you?" The answer to that question is almost always "fine." Open your sentence with words like "when," "how," "why," and "tell me" instead of "do" and "are." If you notice a ring on someone's finger, ask questions like, "Where did you and your husband get married?" "Does that location hold significance to you two?" Wording open-ended questions opens you up to learning more about why someone may choose something different than you! If you see someone with a lot of children, ask them, "Tell me about your kids." Or maybe you know a family with just one child, and you're curious about that: "What did your husband say when he found out you were having a boy?" These are conversation starters. The more that you learn about another person, the more you can start to hand out grace with ease. The awesome thing about this tactic is that even the most introverted person can ask one simple question. People love sharing about themselves. You may find that with just a simple question, people you assumed were shy and introverted were just waiting for someone to care enough to listen.

I'll call my friend Fiona. She was twenty-two when we met, and our lives were worlds apart. We met at an event at my church called "Imagine." Imagine is a one-day event where our local church hosts a bazaar for those going through hardships. People shop—for free—for coats, food, and toys to get their family through the holidays and winter months. The hope is that they come for the toys and leave with Jesus in their lives. Each person who is registered is assigned a host who is a member at our church. I wasn't sure I wanted to host this particular year because only a few days earlier I had returned from my first mission trip to Haiti, and quite simply, I was exhausted. However, something called me there anyway. I knew that the poor I had just seen in Haiti weren't going to compare to the poor people who would show up here. They were lucky enough to have a government that would provide basic needs with food and temporary housing, unlike what I had seen the previous week in Haiti. But God was about ready to open my eyes about what "basic needs" really were. Fiona and I met at the entrance to the church, and I did as I was instructed and sat down with this young black girl to pray with her. If I am being totally transparent, I would have never given this girl a second look in a normal public setting. The musty smell of her jacket, her tight acid washed jeans, and her blue eyeliner would have been a good indicator that she and I were not made for connection. As I prayed a very nervous, rehearsed prayer for this girl, I started seeing tears run through her clumpy, false eyelashes. She excused herself into the bathroom. She was gone for a long time. I was frustrated standing outside of that bathroom door, assuming this girl was up to no good. Was she snorting a line? Was she popping a pill? I was more frustrated because, from the looks of her belly, I thought it was possible that she was pregnant. My anger melted away as she came out of the bathroom with puffy eyes and said, "I'm so sorry; it's just that I've heard people pray at church before, but no one has ever prayed just for me." Conviction hit me like a ton of bricks, and my heart broke and fell in love with this girl all at the same time. "Who will you be shopping for today?"

She responded, "My four children."

Clearly a meeting put together only by God. Fiona and I, although I was thirteen years her senior, had the same number of children at the time, and they were within months of one another in age. I found out later that Fiona's pregnant looking belly was an illusion created by ill-fitted clothing. Just another public service announcement to remind you to never ask a woman when she is due unless you know without a doubt that she is in fact due!

The two of us laughed as we shared stories about our children and how crazy life is when you have four children in four years. We shopped for her kids, we picked out coats and wrapping paper, and when we finished, she looked at me so sincerely and said, "Thank you." I reminded her that I did nothing. The church donated all the items. She said, "No. Thank you for respecting me. Peoples, they look at me like I's a monster now, and you respected me." She hugged me and was on her way. I didn't fully understand what she meant; I probably never will. But my heart was forever changed in knowing she didn't come to the church that day for food, coats, or toys. She could have gotten those things at any local shelter. She came that day to experience a brief moment of love, hope, and respect. To think that, at first, I didn't even want to give her those things because I assumed she was not worthy of them—*as if I had the authority to decide who was worthy of those gifts!* I wonder how often my busy schedule, my obsession with vanity, or my pure self-ishness cause me to overlook someone who simply just needs to feel seen and valued, even if only for a moment.

A few weeks later, I got Fiona's contact information and gave her a call. I didn't realize, at the time, how rare it was for Fiona to not only keep the same phone number for that many weeks but to also answer an unknown number. In hindsight, the connection we made had God's hands all over it. I asked Fiona if I could take her to a nice lunch. She suggested Arby's. Perspective is everything. I knew that she wouldn't be comfortable in what I considered a nice restaurant, but I was able to convince her she'd probably like Chili's. She was over-the-moon excited! "This is the best shrimp I've ever eaten," she exclaimed. Her excitement was like that of a young child on Christmas morning. It tickled me to hear her enthusiasm, which also reminded me of how privileged my life really was.

During our lunch, I found out that Fiona's children were in foster care because she had physically abused them. That's the story you would have heard on the news. Headlines would have said something like, "Woman beats six-year-old daughter because she is an unfit mother." The story I heard was one of heartbreak, a story of a thirteen-year-old girl (Fiona) whose mother died of a drug overdose. Fiona's stepfather "took care of her" by repeatedly raping and beating her. When he finally got her pregnant at the age of sixteen, he kicked her out on the streets of inner-city Chicago, where she found a pimp to take care of her. She loved her pimp because he was the only man who had ever taken good care of her. But when he, too, got her pregnant, he kicked her, her daughter, and their unborn child out on the streets. She decided to make a change and moved to the central part of the state where she could start over. She was eighteen and had two children. She moved in with family but quickly found a boyfriend who gave her two more children. She said, "Well, I think that both of my two little kids are his. I got raped one night, so I am not sure if one of them is his or not."

When I asked her why her children didn't live with her any-more, she hung her head in shame and said, "I didn't know how else to discipline her." By "her," she was referring to her six-year-old daughter. She saw the little girl touching her four-year-old son's penis, likely out of curiosity, and it reminded her of how she was abused as a child. In order to protect all of them from the sin she had been exposed to, she felt the need to "discipline" her daughter. Fiona beat her daughter, and she beat her badly.

I have been over this story in my mind and heart a million times. I have tried making Fiona the monster. I have tried not to love her because a little bitty girl was abused. It's heartbreaking. But what I was given was the gift of Fiona's smile before I heard the story. I got a moment of her tender heart while I prayed with her. I got to see who she was—loved and respected—something that had never happened in her life prior to that day. Fiona never asked me for anything. Not money, not lunch, not clothing, but she would call me sometimes and tell me that she missed me. Always calling me from a different phone number than the one before. She would call me her "bff" and promise me that when she got a job, she would take me out for lunch like I had taken her. I love Fiona, even though there is nothing she did or gave me to "earn" my love. Just like Jesus loves me—and I've done nothing to earn it.

I have five children, four of which are the same ages as Fiona's. But unlike Fiona, I was raised in a loving home. I know what it feels like to be cherished as a daughter and respected as a woman. Still, there were (are!) days when I have to use every single self-soothing coping mechanism I've learned to keep from losing my ever-loving mind with my kids. I've put myself in time out, I've left the house, I've hid in my bedroom where I've devoured a giant bag of chocolate chips. You gotta do what you gotta do! But I have never considered relieving my stress or addressing a discipline problem by delivering a fist to my child's face. I don't excuse what Fiona did. I know for a fact that the judges made the right choice by taking those sweet babies from her and eventually placing them permanently with a loving family to break the cycle of abuse. But no matter how hard I try, I cannot see Fiona as a monster.

I haven't seen or heard from Fiona in a while. She kind of disappeared. I guess that's what you do when you are broken that badly; you try to fade away. She and I had a sweet season of friendship. I am not sure if my friend knows how much our friendship taught me about how Jesus loves me. You see, our sin isn't on a sliding scale. Beat your child or judge someone by their appearance; Jesus hates it all. But the gift is that He forgives it all too.

It doesn't matter what I've done or how bad I yelled at my kids, even if I used a few

> **Beat your child or judge someone by their appearance; Jesus hates it all. But the gift is that He forgives it all too.**

four-letter words. (It happens; I'm human.) Jesus hates all my sin, but He loves me.

Why am I quick to believe what the Bible says about my sin but slow to believe what it says about my forgiveness? My dear friends, as we come to the end of our time together, I hope you will start to see your forgiveness as freedom. We get to be made new each day, actually each second. Jesus greets us each minute with respect, love, and a clean slate. What an incredible gift we have been given.

It's your turn to start choosing forgiveness over fear, opportunity over obligation, and grace over guilt. Until we meet again, my prayer for you is that your vision of the world around you is just a little bit clearer because the FOG that once surrounded you has been lifted.

Endnote

Chapter 3

1 Stern, Joanna. "Cellphone Users Check Phones 150x/day and Other Internet Fun Facts." *ABC News.* May 29, 2013. abcnews. go.com/blogs/technology/2013/05/cellphone-users-check-phones-150xday-and-other-internet-fun-facts/.

Chapter 5

1 Furr, Nathan. "How Failure Taught Edison to Continually Innovate." *Forbes.* June 9, 2011. forbes.com/sites/nathanfurr/2011/06/09/how-failure-taught-edison-to-repeatedly-innovate/#53a5da7765e9.

Chapter 7

1 "32 Shocking Divorce Statistics." *McKinley Irvin Family Law.* October 30, 2012. mckinleyirvin.com/family-law-blog/2012/october/32-shocking-divorce-statistics/#_ednref3.

Chapter 10

1 "She-Ra." Wikipedia. April 1, 2019. en.wikipedia.org/wiki/She-Ra.
2 "He-Man." Wikipedia. March 29, 2019. en.wikipedia.org/wiki/He-Man.
3 Wallace, David Foster. *Infinite Jest.* New York: Back Bay Books, 2009.

About the Author

Lindsey Hale is a courageous storyteller who shares her heart through authentic and transparent stories about faith, marriage, parenting, and leadership. With more than a decade of experience as a top leader with Thirty-One Gifts, Lindsey has a passion for empowering women. She speaks right from the heart in a direct and fun-loving way that is both encouraging and refreshing!

Made in the USA
Middletown, DE
17 May 2019